## What People Are Saying About
### *Four Faces of a Leader* . . .

Leaders ask probing but appropriate questions. Here, Bob Rhoden raises questions that provoke us to cultivate our highest and best quality of leadership character. I'm sending a copy to my pastor!

**JOHN ASHCROFT**
*Former Governor, US Senator, and US Attorney General*

Few people understand the ins and outs of ministry better than Bob Rhoden. *Four Faces of a Leader* is Bob at his best: biblically grounded, spiritually insightful, and eminently practical. I cannot recommend it highly enough. Every minister needs to have these four faces!

**DR. GEORGE O. WOOD**
*General Superintendent, Assemblies of God*

Every once in a while a messenger comes along who can change the course of life for those who embrace his message. Bob Rhoden is such a messenger. With skill and grace he provides four

pillars for leaders to live by that have the potential to transform those we lead. I am one of those changed by his message.

RICK COLE
*Senior Pastor, Capital Christian Center, Sacramento, CA*

*Four Faces of a Leader* provides what this generation of leaders desperately needs. Dr. Rhoden has built a bridge from his generational wisdom to our sometimes fatherless generation. As you read the practical leadership truths, you will feel as if you have your own personal mentor. Thank you, Dr. Rhoden, for being real!

JASON BYARS
*Planter and Lead Pastor,*
*Coastline Community Church, Melbourne Beach, FL*

In this book, I felt like I was sitting down over a fresh cup of coffee with a choice man of God, gleaning insights from his remarkable public and private life. I was challenged, inspired, informed, and encouraged. Without a doubt, I will commend this book to anyone, whether on the first or fiftieth year of their leadership journey.

DR. DON MEYER
*President, Valley Forge Christian College, Phoenixville, PA*

Bob Rhoden is a statesman in the Lord's church. He is a leader of leaders and a pastor to pastors. He has been both sage and friend to me personally. When you read this book, be prepared to see Jesus and leadership in a way you have never seen them before.

**BRYAN JARRETT**
*Lead Pastor, Northplace Church, Sachse and Garland, TX*

*Four Faces of a Leader* is written by one who knows about leadership from a depth of experience. It rings with authenticity, as does Bob Rhoden himself. I am convinced that Bob has discerned correctly the central leadership priorities Jesus demonstrated through His missional service in the gospels. This book will guide and empower you to fulfill your divinely designed calling in that very Jesus-like way.

**DR. KENT J. INGLE**
*President, Southeastern University, Lakeland, FL*

In *Four Faces of a Leader* Dr. Rhoden shares the wisdom of a caring and sensitive heart that has been molded by the Master Shepherd. This book is built on biblical principles that will change the way leaders practice their craft, and change their organizations, institutions, and congregations. This book will challenge all your assumptions about leading God's children.

**ADM. VERN CLARK**
*US Navy (Ret.), Former Chief of Naval Operations*

In this masterpiece, Dr. Rhoden has struck all the right notes. It is a leadership manual and roadmap, a teaching tool that has already begun to influence my life and ministry. The words that come to mind are "a pastor's companion." May you find it to be as valuable a resource as I have.

ST. CLAIR MITCHELL
*Senior Pastor, Evangel Assembly, Temple Hills, MD*

A refreshing, reality-based treatise on Christian leadership as it ought to be. The premise is eye-opening, and the practicality is piercing. Christian leaders would do well to embrace the truths from this book to help bring us back off the edge into a lifestyle of "truth and reason" (Acts 26:25).

DR. BRYAN JOHNSON
*Dean, Seattle Bible College*

*Four Faces of a Leader* is more than a book. It's about a lifestyle of leading people in order to bring out their best. When you apply the "four faces" of leadership to your personal life and your organization, the potential of others becomes your mission! This is a must-read for every leader who desires to be the change the world is looking for.

JESS BOUSA
*Planter and Lead Pastor of Restore Church,*
*Havre de Grace and Perryville, MD*

As I read Bob Rhoden's cogent thoughts, I experienced, in condensed fashion, a lifetime of leadership lessons tempered on the anvil of true servant leadership. This book provides practical, macro insights sure to benefit all ministry leaders.

TERRY L. YANCEY
*District Superintendent, Assemblies of God—Kansas*

# Four Faces of a Leader

---

## WHAT IT TAKES TO MOVE
## YOUR CHURCH FORWARD

Bob Rhoden

with Dean Merrill

## MY HEALTHY CHURCH
MyHealthyChurch.com

Published by My Healthy Church
1445 North Boonville Avenue
Springfield, Missouri 65802

Published in association with The Quadrivium Group—Orlando, Florida
info@TheQuadriviumGroup.com.
Interior design and formatting by Prodigy Pixel. www.ProdigyPixel.com
Cover design by Keith Locke. www.KeithLocke.com

ISBN: 978-1-62423-045-5
Printed in the United States of America
13 14 15 16 • 5 4 3 2 1

# Contents

## PART THREE—THE FACE OF A STEWARD

## PART FOUR—THE FACE OF A SEER

## SUMMARY

# Foreword

I am privileged to call Bob Rhoden a friend, a mentor, and my pastor. He has been all three to me since I first arrived in Washington in 1994. My respect for him as a leader is unequivocal. He is a man of his word and a man of God's Word. He's one of the most authentic people I know, and his wisdom isn't just learned. It's earned.

At critical points in all our lives, we need someone who believes in us more than we believe in ourselves. Bob Rhoden is one of those people to me. His wisdom has helped me navigate challenging seasons. His encouragement has helped me stay the course.

I rarely spend time with Bob that I don't find myself writing down something he says. He makes me think. And I can't remember spending time with him that I'm not inspired to trust God more. His faith is contagious.

I still remember the first time I heard Bob share about the four faces of a leader. I knew immediately that it was a book he had to write. And I consider it a high privilege to write the foreword. While it may only take a few hours to read, these pages contain a lifetime of leadership lessons. For many of you, this book will become like a good friend. It will impact you so profoundly that you'll put it on a shelf that allows easy access. You'll return to the paragraphs and pages that are leafed and underlined.

This book will not just answer questions. It will raise new questions. In fact, it will answer questions you haven't even asked yet. *Four Faces of a Leader* speaks not only to where you are as a leader, it prepares you for the next step in your personal development.

I believe you'll be a better leader having read this book.

I think you'll also find a new friend, my friend, Bob Rhoden.

**MARK BATTERSON**
*Lead Pastor, National Community Church, Washington, DC, and bestselling author*

# Introduction

B efore I start pontificating on what leadership means, you deserve to know who's doing the talking in this book. Let me introduce myself.

I grew up without much leadership, at least in the conventional sense. No dad and no mother after a drunk driver killed her when I was just two years old—only a loving grandmother who did the best she could for me on a tiny government pension. (For the full story, see the appendix.) It's rather amazing, I suppose, that I ended up becoming a pastor.

For twenty-two years my wife and I planted and continued to lead a church in Virginia's capital city. Thereafter I was asked to be a district superintendent, a "pastor to pastors" across the Potomac area. Along the way, I've always tried to study what makes leadership work, how it functions, and who are the best models.

Here are three concerns I carry about myself as a leader:

1. That my ministry career might somehow substitute for my personal relationship with God. I really do not want that to happen. The

truth is, what we all do in church ministry is not necessarily conducive to staying fresh in our spiritual walk.

2. That my ministry might be crippled by distortions I don't recognize—for example, a controlling tendency, or insecurity, or personal fears that bind me. That's why I give permission to people around me to talk with me about what I'm not seeing.

3. That I might succeed in things that don't actually matter. Dr. Leonard Sweet (Drew Theological School) is famous for saying that when we lie down to sleep at night, we should ask, "What did I do today that was worth Christ dying for?" I don't want to climb any ladder only to find that it's leaning against the wrong wall.

I believe in taking these areas seriously. As Paul wrote, "Examine yourselves to see whether you are in the faith; test yourselves" (2 Cor. 13:5).

I'm also concerned, as I watch the contemporary American church, about three additional things:

1. That we will *professionalize* the ministry. Yes, I believe in doing things well. But this is more than a profession, a career.

2. That we will *institutionalize* the church. It's not just an organization to be tweaked by a bunch of engineers. It's organic, dynamic.

3. That we will *secularize* our theology. Of course I'm in favor of being friendly and understandable to guests . . . but if that means adjusting our theology to suit them, to fit the culture, we are on a dead-end track. There will always be a certain amount of tension in the Christian message that cannot be erased. "The offense of the cross" (Gal. 5:11) is unavoidable.

While I believe that healthy churches grow, this book is not a collection of growth strategies for pastors. There's a golf commercial that says, "Bobby Jones worked on his swing, not his score. That is how he became the best golfer of his generation." As leaders we must work on our swing. The score will then take care of itself.

So this is where I'm coming from, personally speaking. I invite you to join me in examining the four faces of a Christian leader. The work of God deserves no less than the best we can give to it. This is a high calling—and a high privilege. I hope you find benefit in the pages to come.

# CHAPTER ONE

# So What Is a Leader?

How do you know if you're an effective Christian leader? I've spent all my adult life as either a pastor or a "pastor to pastors," and I can tell you that if your gauges are like most others in the ministry today, you approach this question by first checking the attendance chart. "How many are coming on Sunday morning?" you ask yourself. "What's my percentage of increase compared to last year? Is my church known in the community as 'growing'?" That's the initial measure of effectiveness.

Next, you look at your church's financial record. "Are all the bills paid? Have we stayed on budget? Will the fiscal year end in the black?"

Then, you go on to the real-estate page. "Is the facility in reasonably good shape? Have we built enough space for all the programs that are running? Is the sanctuary large enough? Do the young people have the rooms they need?"

Such responses are reasonable enough. However, this is sort of like my going to the doctor, who comes into the little room and asks, "So how are you doing, Bob?" If I answer, "Well, I'm making such-and-such a salary, and I'm this many years old, and the market value of my house is currently X hundred thousand dollars . . . " I would be wasting his time. I could be dying of cancer, and he wouldn't know it without somehow getting better data out of me.

He has his own way of determining if I'm okay or not. He takes my blood pressure, he listens to my chest sounds through a stethoscope, he looks down my throat and into my ears, he sends blood samples to the lab, he performs many other tests . . . all to determine how I'm really doing.

In evaluating my effectiveness as a Christian leader, what if I measured myself by standards that told the real truth? For example, am I passionate about holding true to my original calling? Am I regularly doing acts of practical service? What's the honest state of my competence in the ministry? How good am I at casting vision and bringing about necessary change? These would tell much more than a weekly head count or dollar total.

My wife and I lived for a long time less than twenty miles from the Library of Congress, those three magnificent buildings in the middle of Washington, DC, that house the largest collection in the world. Some 32 million books are catalogued there; nearly 2 million people come to visit each year. No wonder the annual budget of the Library of Congress is in the neighborhood of $650 million.

If you delve into the holdings of this amazing collection, which world leader do you think commands the most shelf space? George Washington? Abraham Lincoln? Franklin D. Roosevelt? General George Patton? Actually, it may surprise you to learn that this auspicious place holds more books about Jesus Christ than any other person. He is, in fact, the most riveting leader of all time.

That confirms my inclination to use Him as a benchmark for effectiveness. In just thirty-three years He accomplished more that has lasted longer with greater

> **Jesus Christ is, in fact, the most riveting leader of all time.**

impact and wider reach than any leader in history. Even though, in the words of the well-known essay we preachers like to quote, "He never wrote a book, He never held an office, He never went to college, He never traveled two hundred miles from the place where He was born," yet the truth about Jesus cannot be refuted: "All the armies that ever marched, and all the navies that ever were built, and all the parliaments that ever sat . . . have not affected the life of man upon this earth as powerfully as has that *One Solitary Life*."[1]

How did He do it?

• • • • •

First of all, Jesus viewed Himself as a *shepherd* (Greek: *poimēn*). He knew exactly what He was called to do. The true shepherd focuses on the sheep, He said in John 10. Their potential is the shepherd's sole mission. The true shepherd stays with this mission rather than looking for ways to advance his personal career.

To be an effective Christian leader, I have to function within the borders of my calling. The point is not to move up some ladder; it is to fulfill what God has ordained for me to do.

During my fifteen years as a district superintendent, I made it a point to travel to each of the more than 300 churches under my care across the states of Maryland, Virginia, and northern West Virginia, plus the District of Columbia. It was not enough for me to focus on the thriving, cutting-edge congregations of metro Baltimore, Washington, Richmond, or Norfolk. I remember driving up to a small white clapboard church in the West Virginia mountains where the pastor, Brady Goldizen, was what we politely call "bi-vocational," meaning he had to hold another job in order to make ends meet. Yet he served that church for many years, even though it meant driving forty miles each way from the town where he worked in construction.

> **The real shepherd loves the sheep even when they are ugly, when they bite, when they disobey.**

There didn't seem to be a wife by his side. So at lunch after the service that Sunday, I gently asked about his family situation. With misty eyes, he replied, "Well, let me tell you the story. Many years ago, my wife left me—with a three-year-old daughter to raise by myself. In the early days of my ministry here, the church had no nursery, of course. I would sometimes have to stand in the pulpit holding my daughter in one arm while I held my Bible in the other as I preached.

"She's all grown up now, still serving the Lord, I'm proud to say. And I'm still serving this same church. Retirement is getting closer these days—I don't know how much longer I can continue. But I've been faithful to my calling. I love these people."

This congregation numbered less than fifty folks on an average Sunday. But was this man an "effective Christian leader"? Absolutely. He functioned within the parameters of his calling to be a shepherd. He loved those sheep. He was willing to lay down his very life for them.

The real shepherd loves the sheep even when they are ugly, when they bite, when they disobey. If they run off, he goes and gets them. He makes the ultimate sacrifice.

The extent to which we are devoted shepherds has a lot to do with our effectiveness.

. . . . .

Jesus, the world's greatest leader, also called Himself a *servant* (Greek: *doulos*). On the night of the Last Supper, He got down on His knees and washed the disciples' feet, even though at least one of them found it inappropriate. This is perhaps the only time during His years on earth that He used Himself as an example. He said, "I have set you an example that you should do as I have done for you. I tell you the truth, no servant is greater than his master, nor is a messenger greater than the one who sent him" (John 13:15–16).

This part of Christian work has to do with our character. To possess a humble character will not by itself qualify you for the ministry—but the lack of it will certainly torpedo what you hope to do in ministry.

**Learning to be a true servant is absolutely critical for anyone in leadership.**

Over each of the last few years, I've had the privilege to guide groups of eight students at Valley Forge Christian College—four men, four women—in what's called an "Innovative Leadership Experience." I go up to the campus outside Philadelphia a couple of days in the fall and talk with them about the topic. Then in the spring, I bring them to Washington. I introduce them to an all-star cast of Christian leaders. For example, we walk into the Capitol, go through security, and crowd into the third-floor office of Rear Admiral Barry Black, chaplain of the US Senate. We listen to him tell how God has called him, at this station of life, to this place. "I'm just a servant of God here," he says. But of course, the students can hardly get their eyes off his prestigious office, his massive library, and his stunning view down the Mall toward the Washington Monument.

By that evening, though, I take them across the Potomac to Arlington Assembly of God, where we spend an hour standing behind counters of hot food, dishing up meals for the homeless. These people's clothes are hardly fashionable to collegiate eyes; some of them don't exactly smell the best. They have nothing; they live on the streets, and this is quite likely their only meal for the day.

Yet without fail, the students report back each year, "That Friday night taught me so much about leadership. We began with the high and mighty in the morning, and we ended by serving the lowest and least at night."

Learning to be a true servant is absolutely critical for anyone in leadership. If we could fill in our own report cards, how would we grade ourselves on servanthood? Do other people see our servant face? When people wanted to make Jesus a king, He refused. He came instead as the suffering servant.

· · · · ·

Jesus also showed the face of a *steward* (Greek: *oikonomos*). This is about our competence. Do you think the carpenter's shop at Nazareth ever turned out a crooked drawer? Jesus was careful about what He did. He never let Himself quit halfway along. We can hear Him saying on the cross, "It is finished" (John 19:30). He had done what He came to do.

Jesus was not competitive or jealous. He didn't compare Himself to others. He was too busy being a good steward. And He expects the same from us. We are to take conscientious care of what He entrusts to us.

Jesus voluntarily laid aside His royalty, never complaining. And yet we got the best He had to offer. The temple guards said of Him, "No one ever spoke the way this man does" (John 7:46). In the same way, we are to give our best, wherever we are, whatever we have to work with. As the old saying goes, "holy sloppy" is still sloppy.

When the British colonizers first came to Calcutta, India, they wished for a way to keep playing their beloved game of golf. So they built a course. What they didn't count on was the monkeys coming out of the trees and having a good time picking up their golf balls during a game. The player might tee off with a nice drive down the middle of the fairway, but before he could get to the lie, a monkey would scoop up the ball and drop it into a sand trap or behind a tree.

The golfers tried trapping the monkeys, but to no avail— others quickly arrived to take their place. A fence was erected around the course, which only entertained the monkeys all the more; they loved jumping over it.

Finally, there was no choice but to make a new rule for this particular golf course: *Play the ball where the monkey drops it.*[2]

That's how it is in leadership. You can be sure that even when you hit the ball straight in ministry, some monkey is bound to come along and move it. Things may not go the way you wish, you may not always have everything you need—but you must forge ahead regardless. Competent stewards do the best with what they have and use it to the fullest.

· · · · ·

Finally, Jesus was called a prophet, a *seer* (Greek: *prophetes*). He was the greatest change agent who ever lived. It was not easy for Him; "he came to that which was his own, but his own did not receive him" (John 1:11). He came into a world filled with conflict. The times in which we live are no more challenging than those Jesus faced.

Today the world is looking for leaders who are not put off by change. We in church leadership need to be asking how we're doing as primary vision casters in the place where we serve. How are we doing as teachers, motivators, and change agents?

Jesus was a transformational leader, and He expects us to be the same. My definition of transformational leadership is "courage in action." It brings about the highest order of change. It aligns vision and resources, creates an organizational culture that fosters serving and nurturing, and empowers people by focusing on their worth and potential.

· · · · ·

In this book, we will explore together these four faces of a leader—the shepherd, the servant, the steward, and the seer. It's tempting, when we head into this kind of evaluation, simply to rearrange our prejudices on the subject and call it "thinking." I want to summon each of you to a leadership journey that can potentially move you from simple survival . . . to success . . . and on to significance.

Hockey great Wayne Gretzky was once asked why he always seemed to be the first player to the puck. "I don't skate to where the puck is," he answered. "I skate to where the puck is going to be."[3] Will we be leaders who skate to where our church or organization is going to be in the twenty-first century?

PART ONE

-------------------------------------------------

# The Face of a Shepherd

# CHAPTER TWO

# The Calling

We Americans don't know much about sheep. The top ten sheep-raising countries in the world are: China (128 million of the critters), then Australia (73 million), India (65 million), Iran, Sudan, New Zealand, Nigeria, the UK, Pakistan, Ethiopia . . . and somewhere way, way down the list comes the United States, with only 7 million (maybe). You can hardly find lamb in the meat department of our supermarkets, and we have to import wool from other countries in order to make many of those high-priced coats and sweaters we love.

If we had grown up in the Bible lands, of course, we would know much more about sheep and those who take care of them. They're called *shepherds*. Abraham was one, and so was his son Isaac, and grandson Jacob, as well as many others in the Old Testament, from Abel to Amos. You can add Moses to the list, too, along with Jesse's youngest son; the psalmist writes that God . . .

> chose David his servant
> and took him from the sheep pens;
> from tending the sheep he brought him
> to be the shepherd of his people Jacob,
> of Israel his inheritance.
> And David shepherded them with integrity of heart;
> with skillful hands he led them.
> PS. 78:70–72

That, in a few words, describes our calling in today's church, whether we serve on the plains of eastern Montana (where they still raise sheep) or the gritty streets of Cleveland. We are shepherds. We watch over groups of not-always-bright, not-always-strong creatures. We take care of them anyway, through rain, snow, and gloom of night, providing what they need to become what they were meant to be.

It's not a glamorous job. It doesn't put you among the elite. The smell of sheep trails along behind you most of the time. So why do you do it, Sunday after Sunday, year after year? Because it's your calling.

Like David, we seek to do our work "with integrity of heart." Another way to say that is an *undivided* heart. Our heart integrates all the facets of being called into action that focus on leading the flock. In his book *The Traveler's Gift,* Andy Andrews says, "Most people fail at whatever they attempt because of an undecided heart. Should I? Should I not? Go forward? Go back? Success requires the emotional balance of a committed heart. When confronted with a challenge, the committed heart will search for a solution. The undecided heart searches for an escape.

"A committed heart does not wait for conditions to be exactly right. Why? Because conditions are *never* exactly right. Indecision limits the Almighty and His ability to perform miracles in your life. He has put the vision in you—proceed. To wait, to wonder, to doubt, to be indecisive is to disobey God."[4]

> **All of us should be observing and learning from those we consider effective leaders.**

The part in the psalm about "skillful hands" is about knowing what to do next. Some skills are learned, while others are intuitive. Have you ever asked a leader, "How did you know to do that?" Sometimes the reply will be, "I learned it from a previous experience," or "I can't really tell you. It just seemed to be the obvious thing to do." Effective leaders have both learned skills and intuitive decision-making insights that seem to accrue over time. All of us should be observing and learning from those we consider effective leaders.

As Andrews says in his more recent book, *The Noticer,* "Remember, young man, experience is not the best teacher. *Other people's* experience is the best teacher. By reading about the lives of great people, you can unlock the secrets to what made them great."[5]

The apostle Peter, who grew up on the Sea of Galilee learning a lot more about fish than about sheep, nevertheless turned pastoral when he wrote to church leaders:

To the elders among you, I appeal as a fellow elder.
. . . Be shepherds of God's flock that is under your
care, watching over them—not because you must,
but because you are willing, as God wants you to
be; not pursuing dishonest gain, but *eager to serve;*
not lording it over those *entrusted* to you, but being
*examples to the flock.* And when the Chief Shepherd
appears, you will receive the crown of glory that will
never fade away.

1 PET. 5:1–4, EMPHASIS ADDED

Notice his attention not just to activity but to attitude: "eager to serve." He is saying to his fellow elders that they should seek to add value wherever they are. Leaders do not ask what they can get out of a place, but what they can give to this place. They are focused not on their financial package but on their contribution. They know that if you're truly serving, the church can never afford to pay you what you're worth. If they are paying you what you're worth, you're not working hard enough. We should always be adding value, never just maintaining or subtracting.

Yes, there are challenges to manage in the ministry. There are cantankerous sheep that won't follow directions, that get into the mud, that even bite. But it does no good to whine about them. (They don't understand our language anyway!) We must keep shepherding them.

Why? Because, using Peter's word, they have been "entrusted" to us. We didn't create them, we didn't go out and buy them on the open market, we didn't coax them to come our way; instead, God commended them to our care. At the end of the day, they are His sheep, not ours. They don't need a "lord," says the apostle; they need a caregiver.

And even more, they need an "example" (v. 3). The power of modeling is critical for the sheep. The leader's life needs to be such that people instinctively say, "I want to follow that person. I believe in him."

## A Calling Or a Career?

When Ephesians 4:11–12 says that "Christ himself gave . . . the pastors . . . to equip his people for works of service," the Greek word for pastors is *poimēn*—quite simply, "shepherds" or "feeders." Jesus forthrightly called Himself "the good shepherd" in John 10:11 and went on to say that this entailed "lay[ing] down his life for the sheep." No claim of privilege here, no angling for an easy way out. The Son of God freely took up His calling as a shepherd.

In this lengthy passage in John, Jesus had some stern things to say not only about the "thieves and robbers" who would jump the sheep pen fence in order to "steal and kill and destroy" (John 10:8–10) . . . but also about "the hired hand"— the one who is just doing the job for a paycheck rather than truly caring for the sheep:

> When he sees the wolf coming, he abandons the sheep and runs away. Then the wolf attacks the flock and scatters it. The man runs away because he is a hired hand and cares nothing for the sheep. (VV. 12–13)

If we as church leaders are career-motivated, we will not focus on the sheep at hand; we'll be too busy looking for what will advance our career. We'll constantly be looking out of the corner of our eye to see where the next biggest flock is. If somebody says, "You know, there's a smaller flock over here that needs care," we'll say no thank you.

A call-motivation, on the other hand, responds to the Chief Shepherd, "Lord, I want to be where you want me to be. I will focus on the sheep you've called me to."

Jesus left heaven to come to earth. I don't think it's sacrilegious to say that this was not a "career move." He knew in advance that things were going to get ugly near the end. But He came anyway, because He was *called*. He wanted to please His Father.

I faced a calling versus career dilemma at age twenty-six, as I was finishing up a master's degree in New Testament studies at the prestigious Wheaton Graduate School. I had already graduated from Bible college as well as a liberal arts college, then enjoyed a staff position alongside the well-known David Wilkerson, founder of Teen Challenge. For two years I had traveled the eastern United States speaking to youth audiences that were sometimes extremely large, warning of the perils of drug and alcohol addiction. Following that, I had gone to a youth pastor position at a large Pennsylvania church, pastored by the eminent songwriter Ira Stanphill.

> **Jesus left heaven to come to earth. . . . This was not a "career move."**

Now I would receive my graduate degree. I expected a decent-sized church to snap me up as their lead pastor.

It didn't happen.

My wife, Joan, and I retreated to Virginia, where we had relatives; I found a job driving a delivery truck for a furniture store, just to put food on the table. My career was definitely sputtering. Then we heard about a group of twelve people in Richmond who wanted a pastor to help them start a church in the city's West End. They had no place to meet. They did say, however, that they thought they could scrape up $125 a week in salary. Even in 1969, this was not a lot of money.

But the more we prayed about it, the more Joan and I came to feel that God was *calling* us to this little flock. We said we would come. (We didn't know at the time that, in fact, the group had commitments of only $90 a week. They had told each other they were going to "trust God" for the balance.)

In the first year, 185 first-time guests came into our services. People gave their lives to Christ, were baptized in water, were filled with the Holy Spirit. God began to expand his kingdom in that place.

Early on, I went to a ministers' meeting one day. When the discussion came around to the new church I was starting, a man much more experienced than I—probably in his sixties—looked at me and said, "You work your side of the street, and I'll work mine. Welcome to the ministry!" I was stunned.

To him, I was "the competition." But I couldn't let that attitude govern what I should do or how I should behave. As Bill Hybels says, our competition is not the church down the street; it's any alternative use of time that people have.

Soon a woman who did not attend the church gave us three acres of prime land right on Parham Road, a major artery. By the second anniversary of the church, attendance was averaging above 100. We were doing outreaches to young people with drug issues. It was exciting.

And oh, yes—we never missed a paycheck.

Over the course of the next twenty-two years, more than a thousand of our people went on short-term mission trips to other countries. Numerous young men and women entered preparation for full-time ministry. It became obvious to Joan and me that God had called us to shepherd his people across Richmond.

Calling is not about who has the bigger flock. It is about knowing God's assignment and willingly embracing it.

Success in a *career* is defined by how much you earn and how many people you control. Success in a kingdom *calling* is defined by how much you give away and how many people you serve.

## Working for What?

This is not to imply that the "hired hands" Jesus mentioned do not work hard. They often do sacrifice—for their own advancement. They endure hardship for what it will bring back to them later on.

Shepherds, on the other hand, sacrifice for the sake of the sheep. They know that the true test of their efforts may not be evident until eternity. "Their work will be shown for what it is, because the Day will bring it to light," says 1 Corinthians

3:13–15. "It will be revealed with fire. . . . If what has been built survives, the builder will receive a reward. If it is burned up, the builder will suffer loss. . . ."

What is the motive for our sacrifice? Is it the glory of God, or the advancement of ourselves? The fire will tell whether we have invested in wood, hay, and straw, as opposed to gold, silver, and costly stones. It will show our level of obedience as well as our source of power.

> **Motivation seems to show itself whether we intend it or not.**

Motivation seems to show itself whether we intend it or not. People may be attracted to a local church by its vision . . . but they are maintained by relationships. Sheep, even if not always the brightest of animals, can tell whether they are genuinely appreciated and wanted.

There's an old story of a well-dressed young woman sightseeing in New York City. At one point, the tour passed through a slum area, and the tourist became upset at the sight of a ragged little girl playing in the filthy gutter.

"Look at that child!" she cried. "Why doesn't someone clean her up? Where is her mother?"

"Well," the tour guide explained, "it's this way, miss. The mother loves her child, but she doesn't hate the dirt. You hate the dirt—but you don't love the child. Until love for the girl and hate for the dirt get into the same heart, not much is going to change."

True shepherds love the sheep, even dirty sheep, enough to work for a change regardless of what the clock says. They might have to do it all over again tomorrow. But that's all right. It's part of their calling.

Knowing who we are  drives our commitment. As best-selling authors James Kouzas and Barry Posner say in their book *The Truth about Leadership,* "You cannot fully commit to something that isn't important to you—no one can."[6] My first commitment as a leader must be to value the face of a shepherd.

# CHAPTER THREE

# What Shepherds Actually Do

The shepherd metaphor has a long and distinguished history in Scripture. But now we need to get down to specifics on what it actually entails.

As I think about this in terms of ministry today, four tasks come to mind:

## 1. Feeding

The most obvious task, of course, is that shepherds feed the flock. They search out the right pastures for the sheep. They find fresh water to keep them hydrated. They nurture their growth, so they will make it from day to day.

Providing the congregation's nutrition is our primary job as leaders. Without it, people won't survive spiritually. The men and women we serve are looking for fresh, nourishing

**The Word of God is what changes people. Not our words.**

food. What they most want to know when they walk into the building on Sunday is, *Do you have a word from the Lord for me?*

The best Bible verse I know on good preaching is Nehemiah 8:8, which says, "They read from the Book of the Law of God, making it clear and giving the meaning so that the people understood what was being read." That's it, all in one sentence. God's Word is the eternal, priceless Truth; it's what we all need to live. Now, will anybody make it clear and give the meaning so that folks in the seventh row actually "get it"?

It is easier to preach "truths" than the Truth. If you just chase topical "truths," you will run out of things to say. The Truth of the Bible is what we must proclaim. We are not smart enough to concoct stand-alone "meals" week after week on our own. If we try, we end up serving "fast food"—actually, junk food.

And the sheep deserve better.

The Word of God is what changes people. Not our words. His. The Bible is, in fact, the one book in the world whose Author is present every time you read it. He helps us understand its words of life.

Feeding the Truth to a congregation requires advance planning. It took me awhile in the ministry to realize that people could not remember fifty-two miscellaneous things each year. I gradually came to ask God for one theme from Scripture, usually one book, that I could stay with for at least a month. The first law of learning is repetition. I learned to strike the same nail again and again until I could drive it deep into the wood.

Yes, I know that sermon preparation can get tedious after a while. The weekly requirement starts to feel monotonous. But the same could be said by any mother in her kitchen. "What, they're hungry again?" Yes. Feeding is a necessity of life.

Sometimes we get distracted with the systems and add-ons that surround our feeding work. The late evangelist Tom Skinner used to tell ministers to take a sheet of paper and draw a line down the middle. The left half he labeled "Ministry," while the right half he labeled "Monster." Then he would say:

"If on the left side you write something like, 'Two people came to Christ,' then you're tempted to write on the right, 'Now I need a newsletter to tell people about this.'

"If you write, 'Fifteen kids are now coming to the youth group,' you'll want to add, 'We need a van to transport them.'

"If you write, 'Preached three good sermons' on the left, it leads to 'I need to market these to other preachers.'"

Then Skinner would make his real point: "If you're not careful, the Monster will eat your lunch. You'll get so involved in the Monster side that you lose the Ministry side. Granted, both sides are necessary. But don't let the Monster control you. Focus on the left; that's what drives the right."

In the process, if your attention is riveted on nourishing the flock, you may find God supplementing your "menu" with things you hadn't planned to serve at all. I well remember one Sunday morning in January when I intended to set the congregational tone for the coming year. My sermon notes were prepared. But suddenly, I felt an impression from the Holy Spirit. I began to say, "I know that some of you have situations of hurt in your life. You may be here this morning and you're thinking about having an abortion." (Where did *that* come from? Certainly not from my mind!) "And you're struggling about what to do.

"I want you to know that you're in a place this morning where we love you and care for you. We would be most willing to pray for you as you sort this out. I'm saying this not because it was in my plans for today, but because I just felt I should."

That same week, the phone rang in my office. A young student at the University of Richmond introduced herself and said she had been in the service. She wanted to come see me.

We sat down together, and she spilled the whole story . . . how she had been a person of faith, but she had strayed during college and was now pregnant. "I need to get my life straightened out with the Lord," she admitted. "I have to decide whether to marry this guy or not."

She renewed her faith in Christ that day. She carried through with the pregnancy. I ended up performing the wedding of this couple. I'm glad to report that they are still strong in their Christian walk today, a number of years later.

The Spirit led a shepherd to address an issue he wasn't even thinking about. But one of the scared, vulnerable sheep desperately needed it.

## 2. Adding Value

In all that shepherds do for the flock, they seek to add value to their lives, to bring them into a healthy state, to guide them toward maturity.

There should be no "fleecing" of the sheep, even when a word of correction is necessary. When we preach, we must talk the way we would like others to talk to us. When I speak to young pastors, I often use the phrase "Your potential is my mission." That's how I honestly feel. I want them to become all they can be.

The apostle Paul contended constantly for the *unity* of the church. He didn't spend much time throwing people out! He wanted to "equip [the] people for works of service, so that the body of Christ may be built up until we all reach unity in the faith and in the knowledge of the Son of God" (Eph. 4:12–13).

The Greek word for "equip" (other translations say "prepare" or "train") is actually *katartismon,* which comes from the verb *katartizein.* The word has a medical meaning of setting a fracture so it can heal. People come to us in a broken state. Our teaching and preaching should apply a cast, as on a broken arm that needs to heal for a time before it is used again.

*Katartismon* has a couple of other meanings. One is to reconcile factions, to heal the divisions in a group. Yet another use of the word can be to mend a torn fishing net. People's lives get torn and need the restoring touch of God's messenger. Galatians 6:1 encourages us to be gentle when we "restore" a person caught in a sin.

That is why we set up special ministries in our churches for divorce recovery, among other things. Cleansing Stream is yet another approach that seeks to wash out the bondages from believers' lives.[7]

It would not be far off the mark to translate Ephesians 4:11–12 this way: "Christ himself gave the apostles, the prophets, the evangelists, the pastors and teachers, to *mend* (or to *restore*) his people for works of service. . . ."

The passage then goes on to point toward "becom[ing] *mature*, attaining to the whole measure of the fullness of Christ. Then we will no longer be infants, tossed back and forth by the waves, and blown here and there by every wind of teaching. . . . Instead, speaking the truth in love, we will grow to become in every respect the *mature* body of him who is the head, that is, Christ" (vv. 13–15, emphasis added).

What is maturity? My definition is, when people produce more than they consume. If sheep are healthy, they will reproduce. They will have the capacity to bring new lambs into the world. Their earlier wounds and weaknesses are mended, and now they are able to contribute.

This is the kind of value we shepherds seek to add to our flock. It doesn't happen all at once. It's a process.

Dick Foth, a good friend of mine who's been a pastor, a college president, and then a behind-the-scenes mentor to powerful people all across Washington, DC, says, "We tend to think we can disciple people into maturity by events," meaning big, dramatic meetings. "We should instead seek to engage them in the process of discipleship." It takes longer. But it also lasts longer.

He also says, "If you want to go somewhere fast, you go alone. But if you want to go far, you go together. The church is called to go far. It takes longer—but that's all right."

Sheep, after all, are not cheetahs. They lumber along slowly. They need patient shepherds who take the long view of things.

# 3. Bonding

Obviously, this requires spending large blocks of time with the sheep. That's the only way to get to know them and what they need.

Shepherds don't just treat a sheep's occasional illness, like a veterinarian, and then jump back in their pickup truck to drive away. They live with their sheep. Jesus said, "I know my sheep and my sheep know me" (John 10:14). In that, He was reflecting the advice of Proverbs 27:23—"Be sure you know the condition of your flocks, give careful attention to your herds."

One of my mentors, Dr. Robert Cooley, is a prominent evangelical scholar and archaeologist who has led many excavations in the land of Israel. He tells about visiting a shepherd outside Anathoth (Jeremiah's village) named Abdullah. They talked on toward twilight and longer, until it was dark. Seated around the fire, Abdullah then said, "Excuse me, but I need to bring the sheep into the fold for the night."

Dr. Cooley watched as he moved among his sheep, feeling the heads of the ewes and lambs. When Abdullah returned to the campfire, the visitor asked what he had been doing. "I was matching up the right lambs to their mothers," he explained. "I know my sheep, even in the dark, by the shape of their heads."

**Sheep need patient shepherds who take the long view of things.**

I'm always suspicious of ministers who zip off the platform at the closing amen and disappear. What is so distasteful about simply being with the people? They want someone to hear their worries ("Would you pray for my nephew? He's being deployed to the Middle East this week") and also their joys ("Guess what, Pastor? We sold our house after all this time!"). I sometimes stood in the foyer with a tape recorder in my pocket (Is that legal?) so I would be sure to remember who said what, and I could send them a note or an e-mail afterward.

Yes, I'm aware that in a larger congregation one shepherd cannot know all the people. However, caring systems can be developed so that all the people have access to a trained leader. If nurturing is one of our core values, how can we overlook (or dare I say, neglect) this opportunity to show the face of a shepherd?

One of the things pastors of larger churches tend to forget is that a segment of the congregation was there when it was smaller. These people helped bear the burden of getting the church launched. Make sure you do not abandon them when they need your care, no matter how large the congregation grows. The Twelve always had a special relationship with Jesus even as the crowds following Him swelled into the thousands.

On the other hand, every individual has value. The apostle James wrote about not preferring rich people over poor people. It's easy, especially when the church needs money or talented workers, to start looking for people with certain assets. The test, however, is what Abraham faced up on Mount Moriah (Gen. 22)—would he totally trust God as his source, or not? If God is truly all we need, then it doesn't matter if Donald Trump walks into your church or not.

The most condemned sin in the Bible is idolatry, which is what? It is seeking to make the invisible visible. You and I tend to put our trust in visible things rather than the invisible God. This is a test for everyone but especially for leaders who are, as we like to say, "trying to get to the next level."

To the members of a flock, whether wealthy or poor, the pastor's support is spelled p-r-e-s-e-n-c-e. How can we lead the sheep if we're not with them? That presurgery visit to the hospital is important. You represent God to the person who's about to go under the knife or laser. Take time to read Psalm 121 to them, especially verse 8 (NKJV): "The Lord shall preserve your going out [to the operating room] and your coming in [back into your hospital room] from this time forth, and even forevermore." I've read that Scripture in dozens of hospital wards over the years, and it has always been a comfort.

If we're too busy to do this kind of shepherding, we're too busy. The prophet Ezekiel was told to confront the leaders of his time with these words:

> This is what the Sovereign Lord says: Woe to you shepherds of Israel who only take care of yourselves! Should not shepherds take care of the flock? You eat the curds, clothe yourselves with the wool and slaughter the choice animals, but you do not take care of the flock. You have not strengthened the weak or healed the sick or bound up the injured. You have not brought back the strays or searched for the lost. You have ruled them harshly and brutally. . . .
>
> Therefore, you shepherds, hear the word of the Lord: As surely as I live, declares the Sovereign Lord, because my flock lacks a shepherd and so has

been plundered and has become food for all the wild animals, and because my shepherds did not search for my flock but cared for themselves rather than for my flock, . . . I am against the shepherds and will hold them accountable for my flock. I will remove them from tending the flock so that the shepherds can no longer feed themselves. . . . I myself will search for my sheep and look after them.

EZEK. 34:2–4, 7–8, 10–11

Bonding with the sheep is a central part of our calling to be shepherds. It's not just a technique; it's a lifestyle.

This passage even talks about going after the strays who wander off. I know a lot of ministers will say that when people leave a church (which happens all too frequently these days), it's their decision, and just let them go. I disagree. I believe in making one last effort to retain them. You can't force them to come back—but they need to know they're important and that somebody cares about their souls.

Only through close contact over a period of time does a pastor get to know the sheep well enough to discern what's *not* being said, what's bothering them under the surface. I well remember a certain building program to construct a multipurpose facility for our church. Half was to be our worship space, while the other half was a gymnasium. The architect had insisted that the middle wall dividing the two—which formed the backdrop for our platform—should be orange. I tried to talk him out of that color, but he said it fit with the building's overall palette. He was sure he was right.

I observed that people would come into the morning service, sit down facing that orange wall, and start to scowl! Subconsciously it was making them mad (even madder than they already were about the cost overruns on this building). I was sure the color had something to do with their mood. The architect blew that off as nonsense.

Well, all I can tell you is that as soon as the building was complete and he left the premises, we promptly got out the cans and repainted that wall a neutral cream color. The very next Sunday, the congregation seemed more relaxed, even pleasant. It was like we had a new worship space!

Every context is different. Leaders must pick up on the subtleties. I learned over many years that the Richmond culture doesn't do anything explosively. It's not Atlanta, for example. This city proceeds slowly, deliberately. (After all, we've all been here since George Washington's time!) There's a reason why our state song is "Carry Me Back to Old Virginny"—notice, not "the New South." The legislature decided in 1997 that maybe that song, historic as it is, should be replaced with something less tied to the time of slavery . . . but still hasn't gotten around to making a new selection. Things take longer to happen here in Richmond.

This is just one illustration of the need to understand people's context and culture. The more we bond with them, the more we know where they're coming from.

# 4. Protecting

The final thing shepherds do is create a safe place for their sheep. Many predators await on every side, most of which are too strong for the sheep to resist. Among the hazards, says Dr. Kevin Leman in *The Way of the Shepherd,* are these: fear, rivalry, pests, and hunger.[8]

If people are afraid of how the pastor will react to them . . . or how he will speak about them behind their backs . . . they will not feel safe. If a minister is flirtatious or sarcastic, people will question their security. The unprofessional conduct raises doubts about the health of the overall environment.

When religious fads come along, the wise shepherd keeps the people from chasing tangents. This includes being careful about who gets invited to be a guest speaker. Is this someone you can trust to bring nutritious food, or not? Sometimes pastors give their microphone to a speaker who happens to be a longtime friend, or just needs the honorarium. Those are not good enough criteria. The guest must be qualified to deliver genuine benefit to the listeners.

I remember one speaker who came to our church and, in the middle of his message, said something off-base. He referenced David's adultery and pointed out that the 1 Chronicles account skips over that story, unlike in 2 Samuel. He then extrapolated that to mean that our sins can go entirely away; God doesn't even remember them.

This was not just an accidental misstatement of fact, like saying David was from Hebron instead of Bethlehem. This was an error on a central truth of how forgiveness takes place.

Our sanctuary seating was circular back then, so I could see a couple of people looking at me with questioning eyes. In fact, I could feel the whole congregation freezing up.

**When religious fads come along, the wise shepherd keeps the people from chasing tangents.**

In time, he finished his message. I didn't want to stand up and embarrass him right then. I was still pondering how to handle this. But I did speak with him privately afterwards. "What you said this morning on that one point was not biblical," I told him. "You omitted the need for genuine repentance."

He was surprised, to say the least. "I've preached this message several other places, and nobody's ever had a problem with it," he protested.

"Well," I calmly answered, "it's important for me to let you know that we don't teach that here. And I'm going to have to say something about it next Sunday."

A week later I said to the congregation, "Many of you were here last Sunday and heard what our guest said. And you know that isn't what we teach, in accordance with the Bible." I then went on to clarify.

A considerable number of people thanked me afterward. My words had apparently conveyed to them, *This church is a safe place. Our pastor protects us; he cares.*

The same principle applies to what transpires beyond the pulpit—for example, in the exercise of spiritual gifts. At the church in Richmond we defined ourselves as "a Pentecostal church that makes sense," but we still had to manage certain excesses. While many people are well-intentioned, some insist on making a spectacle of themselves. The congregation needs to know that their pastor will guide things appropriately.

Don't misunderstand me; I would be the last person in the world to ever want to "quench the Spirit" (1 Thess. 5:19). Instead I seek to follow the apostle Paul, whose response to any misuse of a gift was not to omit it but to teach about it.

This kind of work sometimes requires courage. You'd rather not cause a wave. But you need to step up for the protection of the flock. When there is disruption or dissension in the fellowship, you cannot just shrug and walk away.

This came to me strongly one day when I was reading in Numbers 16 about the rebellion of Korah and his allies. It was a time of terrible conflict and grumbling against Moses' leadership. Things went from bad to worse, until God finally judged the dissenters in dramatic fashion—which led to further complaints. "You have killed the Lord's people," the crowd said (v. 41). God then unleashed a full-scale plague against them.

In that moment, Moses shouted to his brother, Aaron (the high priest), to take immediate action by hurrying with a censer full of incense and burning coals "'to the assembly to make atonement for them. Wrath has come out from the Lord; the plague has started.' So Aaron did as Moses had said, and ran into the midst of the assembly.... He stood between the living and the dead, *and the plague stopped"* (vv. 46–48, emphasis added).

Leaders who care sometimes have to take the censer of fire God has entrusted to them and head right into the middle of the mess, saying, "I'm here to stop this plague. It will go no farther." And when we do, sighs of relief break out all over.

Protecting the sheep—even from their own stupidity—is part of what shepherds do. We don't seek accolades for this kind of action. We accept it as all in a day's work. Our eyes are fixed on loving these sheep and bringing them to greater and greater realms of maturity and health.

# CHAPTER FOUR

# Sacrifices of a Shepherd

Nobody said that shepherds have a soft life. If you start making a list of the hardships that ministry entails, you quickly identify with the apostle Paul, who wrote his own list in 2 Corinthians 4 about being "hard pressed on every side . . . perplexed . . . persecuted . . . struck down . . . given over to death for Jesus' sake" (vv. 8–11). Our list as modern-day shepherds goes something like this:

## Long (and Odd) Hours

This is not a nine-to-five job. There's a reason why the angelic hosts announced the Christ child's birth late at night to "shepherds abiding in the fields" outside Bethlehem. Most everyone else was asleep by then. But not these guys. They were still working.

Ministry today involves lots of nights and weekends, for the obvious reason that those are the times when people are most available. Beyond that, emergencies have a way of breaking loose at odd hours. Yet there is plenty that needs attention during the work day as well. Some conscientious souls in the ministry have worked so many hours a week that their families and their own health have suffered. But there is no getting around the fact that it's an irregular lifestyle. It always will be.

**Hard work in the ministry doesn't necessarily get you a raise, as in other fields.**

We do get tired sometimes. In the early days of my pastoral ministry, I had three sermon preparations a week: Sunday morning, Sunday night, and Wednesday night. I remember one Sunday night service when, about fifteen minutes into the message, I had to admit I was just flailing away and making little sense. I closed my Bible and said, "You know, folks, I don't really know what I'm trying to say. Let's just gather here at the front and pray for a while." Well, at least I was being honest! I needed to take a couple of days off and rest, in order to come back fresh.

Obviously, you don't want to make that kind of pulpit confession more than once. Better to pace yourself the week before.

## Isolation

The long hours are worsened by the fact that a shepherd works in relative isolation. With 84 percent of American churches being under 200 in attendance, the majority of pastors have a limited team. Their peers and colleagues are not usually around to see their successful moments: those counseling appointments where they gave out a brilliant insight, those messages that truly soared. Like classroom teachers whose awesome pedagogy is seen and heard only by their scruffy students, the minister works without applause.

Every leader knows the feeling of empty space around him or her in the tough decisions of saying no or making budget cuts for the second year in a row or having the board forget to honor Clergy Appreciation Month. It's not fun when you're trying to mediate a dispute in the congregation and *both* antagonists think you're crazy.

## Low Pay

The average evangelical pastor in America earns just $38,000 a year. This is not a profession for the financially ambitious. (In that sense, it's like tending physical sheep; I'm told that most shepherds in North America do it more as a hobby than for a real livelihood.)

Hard work in the ministry doesn't necessarily get you a raise, as in other fields. I've had more than a few sincere ministers come to me and say, "I love my work, and I believe God has called me to this—but I just can't keep up with my bills. My kids are growing up and need more things every year. What am I going to do?" Many of them start looking for a part-time job. Or their spouse gets a job. Or their parents start to subsidize them.

Sometimes those lay leaders who are responsible to set salaries have the mistaken notion that the ministry itself is a reward and pastors don't need to be paid at the same level as other service-oriented professionals. My response is that, while we're not CEOs of profit-making corporations, we are at least equivalent to, say, school principals, who oversee the education of the community's students. Our contribution to the spiritual health of the town is certainly on a par with that.

In the early days of planting the Richmond church, our children qualified for reduced-price lunches at school. We never signed up, however—because we thought it would reflect badly on the church, which was doing the best it could for us with what was coming in.

One day, Joan called and asked me to pick up a short list of groceries on my way home at the end of the day. What she didn't know was that I was basically out of cash, and the checkbook was empty. (We weren't using credit cards in those days.)

I hung up the phone and went upstairs to the sanctuary. I sat in a pew, despondent. "God, I really need your help. I can't even take care of this list," I said, looking down at the paper in my hand.

Just then, though it was a weekday afternoon, a woman walked in. "I've been looking for you," she said. "You spoke at our meeting a few weeks ago, and we just realized we didn't give you an honorarium. I'm so sorry." She handed me an envelope with thirty-five dollars inside.

I've never forgotten that moment. It said to me that when God calls us, He also provides for us. It has helped me to pray (and to recommend) the prayer of Jeremiah 17 that says:

Heal me, Lord, and I will be healed;
save me and I will be saved,
for you are the one I praise
I have not run away from being your shepherd;
you know I have not desired the day of despair.

(VV. 14, 16)

## Facility Cost Challenges

Closely tied to the low-pay situation, and often the cause of it, is not enough money in the congregational coffers. Building programs can become competition for salary increases. Ironically, the pastor who needs a raise is often the one who has cast the vision for a building program.

I remember one difficult season in the 1980s when West End Assembly was struggling. We were in the midst of the building program I mentioned previously, whose costs had gotten far beyond the budget, so that we couldn't keep up. The original estimate of $500,000 was turning out to be closer to $900,000.

At the same time, we were trying to make a governance change in our structure. Opinions were running con as well as pro.

The "faith movement" was at high tide just then, and so some people said our financial squeeze was evidence that we just didn't have "enough faith." Others, however, were more befuddled; instead of coming to church each week expecting anything from God, they sat there evaluating whether we could stay afloat.

One day I was sitting in the pastor's study and . . . just lost it. I broke down and started crying. The secretary grew concerned and called my wife. "You'd better come over and be with Bob," she said softly.

Joan soon arrived. She gave me a long hug. "It's going to be all right, honey," she said. I wasn't so sure.

But I couldn't quite bring myself to "run away from being your shepherd."

A few days later, my two associate pastors—both wonderful men—came in and said, "Bob, we're going to go out and paint houses part-time, the way we used to do in seminary. That way you can stay here and 'mind the store.'"

**Sacrifice has a way of driving something deep down in your soul.**

"No, you're not going anywhere," I responded. "Whatever comes in for salaries we will split three ways. The three of us are not going to run away."

The financial tide eventually turned—when the leadership of the church (pastors, elders, and deacons) stood before the congregation on a Sunday and made a confession. "Let's be honest," we said, "we've made some mistakes. Our hearts have been right, but we've erred in over-committing to this building project. We ask you to forgive us." It was a genuine breakthrough. The people rallied around, and from that point forward, we began seeing more income. While it took another two years to get stabilized, we made it.

Today, one of those young associates, John Hershman, is the senior pastor of West End. The church is strong and vibrant.

For the past fifteen years it has given more than a million dollars annually to missions.

Sacrifice has a way of driving something deep down in your soul. It reinforces that you belong here, God planted you here, and you're not going anywhere else.

## Constant Availability

This is another part of the price of shepherding. The sheep need you when they need you (or at least *think* they need you). The fact that you're on vacation, or sound asleep, is beside the point.

A pastor has to be prepared for the fact that some people don't recognize what is a true emergency. I love the story about Teddy Kollek, the legendary former mayor of Jerusalem:

> [He] once returned home very late, as he often did, and found a note from his wife, Tamar: "A woman rang the doorbell at 1 a.m. to complain that there is a hole in the sidewalk near her house and that the city has done nothing about it for a month." Kollek's home phone number was listed in the telephone book; people could call him at home, and some abused the privilege.
>
> It was 3:30 a.m., and Kollek promptly called the woman back. "This is Teddy," he said. "I just wanted to tell you that tomorrow morning, first thing, I'll deal with the matter."[9]

A delicious story . . . but of course, you can't do that in church ministry.

Nevertheless, I cringe when I hear pastors repeat the old joke, "I'd love the ministry if it weren't for the people." I sometimes respond, "Please don't ever say that again. People are why we're here."

Granted, they can wear you down at times, draining your energy. That is why we need to minister out of a divine anointing not just an awareness of their needs. If all we're doing is working to meet needs, we'll be running twenty-four hours a day. But if our ministry springs out of an anointing, we will awaken each day with the question "What does God want me to do today for whom?"

Peter summarized it well for Cornelius and his family—"God anointed Jesus of Nazareth with the Holy Spirit and power, and . . . he went around doing good and healing all who were under the power of the devil, because God was with him" (Acts 10:38). That's the key to long-term endurance.

## Limited Privacy

Closely related to availability is the fact that ministers have limited privacy. If you're a leader, you're a public figure. Your life and activities are on display for all to see.

So are those of your spouse and children. It simply doesn't work to say, "Well, I'm your pastor, but leave my wife and kids out of this." The only option is to position the work of ministry as a family endeavor, the kind of thing "we do *together*."

Our son, Rob, was co-captain of his high school football team during his senior year. To help build team spirit, he asked his barber to etch the number twelve (his jersey number) on one side of his head, and three stripes on the other side. When he made his grand entrance back at home, I remember the thought that quickly raced through my mind: *What will the church people think about this?* After all, Rob was a leader in the youth group; he'd even gone on a mission trip that summer and had come back telling how it had changed his life.

I knew this was an important moment not only in our father-son relationship but also in helping the church understand how to handle the impetuous actions of teenagers. I reminded myself that there was nothing rebellious in what Rob had done. He was simply trying to be a leader, to fire up his team.

The next Sunday, I prefaced my sermon by saying, "I suppose you've noticed my son's new haircut by now." There was a nervous laugh across the congregation. "I should probably explain to you the spiritual significance of this. The number twelve is for the twelve disciples, and the three stripes represent the Holy Trinity." You guessed it—the place broke out in applause, as Rob grinned sheepishly.

It was a great teaching moment for our church. It said that our family accepted the limited privacy that goes along with being a lead pastor, but we would also protect our children from extraneous criticism.

## High Expectations (Even Perfection)

Naturally, the sheep expect shepherds to know what they're doing, to make good decisions, to keep their word, to act honorably at all times. If we think that's asking too much, then we need to question whether this is truly where we belong.

When people trust our voice and follow us, they are actually affirming our call. They are saying that we have earned the place of leadership. The apostle Paul did not shrink from inviting people to "follow my example, as I follow the example of Christ" (1 Cor. 11:1). "Just as you have us as a model, keep your eyes on those who live as we do," he advised the Philippians (3:17).

In the Kouzes-Posner book mentioned earlier, one of the ten major truths about leadership is this: "You either lead by example, or you don't lead at all." They add that when researchers ask the question "How do you know credible behavior when you see it?" the most frequent answer is this: "You have to do what you say you will do" (abbreviated as DWYSYWD).[10] All of us who are called to be shepherds should stand and salute this expectation every day.

## Negative Feedback

When we fall short—or even when we don't—those who watch us are quick to say so. Being in the ministry is not always popular. Unbelievers have their criticisms, of course, and we understand why. It's harder to take the slings and arrows of those who claim to be Christians.

When George Whitefield, the great British evangelist, preached up and down the eastern seaboard in the 1740s with strong results, not everyone was pleased. A particular critic was Charles Chauncy, the longtime minister of First Church, Boston. He found Whitefield's open-air sermons to be excessively flamboyant.

One day he ran into Whitefield on the street. He knew the evangelist had been making a tour down into the more southern colonies, but now it appeared he was back in Boston.

With an icy tone Chauncy said, "I'm sorry to see you have returned."

Whitefield didn't miss a beat. "So is the devil!" he retorted with a smile, and went on his way. [11]

**When people trust our voice and follow us, they are actually affirming our call.**

We cannot allow the sarcasm of our critics to dissuade us from our calling. God never promised that we would be universally liked. His prophets of old certainly were not. In the end, He is the one we must please.

Moses (who worked as a shepherd for forty years, remember) had hardly gotten the Israelites out onto the road from Egypt before the complaining began. They had not even reached Mount Sinai when, at Rephidim, there was a water shortage.

They grumbled against Moses. They said, "Why did you bring us up out of Egypt to make us and our children and livestock die of thirst?"

Then Moses cried out to the Lord, "What am I to do with these people? They are almost ready to stone me."

The Lord answered Moses, *"Walk on ahead of the people.* Take with you some of the elders of Israel and take in your hand the staff with which you struck the Nile, and go. I will stand there before you by the rock at Horeb. Strike the rock, and water will come out of it for the people to drink." So Moses did this in the sight of the elders of Israel.

EXOD. 17:3–6 NIV 1984, EMPHASIS ADDED

I love that instruction from God: "Walk on ahead of the people." That's what a shepherd does. He does not get down into the bickering. He doesn't get distracted or diverted. He steadily leads toward the solution.

A shepherd's life is not simple. It entails multiple sacrifices. But the rewards in this life—and the life to come—far exceed the sacrifices. As Peter wrote, "When the Chief Shepherd appears, you will receive the crown of glory that will never fade away" (1 Pet. 5:4).

The calendar of my life now shows more days behind me than are ahead. To borrow a line from an old movie, my life has exceeded my dreams. I remain glad that I was entrusted with the care of God's flock.

PART TWO

_____

# The Face of a Servant

# CHAPTER FIVE

# Strange Combination

A t first it was a jolting phrase, an oxymoron like "surfboarding Eskimo" or "320-lb. quarterback." The words *servant leader* just didn't fit together. As a leader, you were the top dog. Concepts such as team, collegiality, 360-degree reviews, and staff feedback were not the DNA of most work environments. The focus was on the power of the leader, not the empowerment of the team.

In fact, if you were a leader, you obviously hired servants (a.k.a. secretaries, assistants, junior staff) to take care of your grunt work and thereby help you succeed in your job, right? As they say in the military, RHIP ("Rank has its privileges").

But in 1970 a well-respected business thinker named Robert K. Greenleaf, veteran of an effective career at AT&T, came out with his essay titled "The Servant as Leader." It didn't appear in the *Harvard Business Review* or other prestigious journal; he had to print 200 copies himself and hand them out to friends and contacts. Soon, however, a buzz began. People were intrigued with such thinking as this (reprinted here from one of Greenleaf's books):

> A fresh critical look is being taken at the issues of power and authority, and people are beginning to learn, however haltingly, to relate to one another in less coercive and more creatively supporting ways. A new moral principle is emerging, which holds that the only authority deserving of one's allegiance is that which is freely and knowingly granted by the led to the leader in response to, and in proportion to, the clearly evident servant stature of the leader.
>
> Those who choose to follow this principle will not casually accept the authority of existing institutions. Rather, they will freely respond only to individuals who are chosen as leaders because they are proven and trusted as servants. To the extent that this principle prevails in the future, the only truly viable institutions will be those that are predominantly servant-led.[12]

Of course, by the time Greenleaf died in 1990, we had all heard his term and gotten used to it. It didn't raise eyebrows anymore. Executives from Wall Street to government to education to the church declared themselves to be "servant leaders," whether they fully grasped the meaning or not. The catchphrase had become almost trendy.

The truth is, however, that Greenleaf didn't invent this idea. It goes back some 2,000 years to the iconoclastic Rabbi who said to His ambitious followers:

> You know that those who are regarded as rulers of the Gentiles lord it over them, and their high officials exercise authority over them. Not so with you. Instead, whoever wants to become great among you must be your servant, and whoever wants to be first must be slave of all. For even the Son of Man did not come to be served, but to serve, and to give his life as a ransom for many.
>
> MARK 10:42–45

We can assume Jesus' listeners that day didn't fully get His point, at least by the way they reacted a week or two later at the Passover meal. The borrowed room they used that evening apparently didn't come with a *servant* to wash everyone's dusty feet before eating. And none of them was about to volunteer for the task.

So their *leader*—the Son of God, no less—decided He would do it. "He got up from the meal, took off his outer clothing, and wrapped a towel around his waist. After that, he poured water into a basin and began to wash his disciples' feet, drying them with the towel that was wrapped around him" (John 13:4–5).

Peter, for one, was totally mystified. He protested that this action was quite out of place, inappropriate. Jesus refuted his protest and went ahead with the washing.

Can you imagine how long this went on? Twenty-four dirty feet, one at a time . . . at least ten minutes, if not fifteen. My curiosity has often wondered whose feet got washed first. And I've speculated that Judas may have been the last, given the notice of betrayal that immediately followed.

When Jesus finished the whole lot of them, he asked a poignant question: "Do you understand what I have done for you?" (v. 12)

Unspoken answer: *Not really.* So He spelled it out:

You call me "Teacher" and "Lord," and rightly so, for that is what I am. Now that I, your Lord and Teacher, have washed your feet, you also should wash one another's feet. I have set you an example that you should do as I have done for you. Very truly I tell you, no servant is greater than his master, nor is a messenger greater than the one who sent him. Now that you know these things, you will be blessed if you do them. (VV. 13–17)

What a bold instruction to us all. Jesus wasn't just putting on an act; He meant for this behavior to continue in the lives and work of His disciples.

He felt entirely comfortable doing this menial service because He was sure of His true place in the hierarchy of things: He "knew that the Father had put all things under his power, and that he had come from God and was returning to God" (v. 3). In other words, He had no worries about status or image. He was confident in Himself as a leader. It wouldn't hurt His reputation to get down on His knees and serve others.

In fact, He had already taken a step down to come from heaven in the first place. Philippians 2 explains that He, "being in very nature God, did not consider equality with God something to be used to his own advantage; rather, he made himself nothing by taking the very nature of a servant, being made in human likeness" (vv. 6–7). Against this backdrop, washing feet was no big deal.

> **Jesus had no worries about status or image. He was confident in Himself as a leader.**

## Who Is Worth Following?

Insecure people have trouble being servants. They worry that they'll get walked on. They say to themselves, "Well, too much of this 'servanthood thing' will undercut my image as a leader. I need to be respected, to have the authority to make tough decisions."

The truth is—as Robert K. Greenleaf pointed out, after studying employee behavior through the turbulent 1960s—the *lack* of servanthood has a way of torpedoing leadership. People don't respect stuffed shirts. They warm up instead to those who are willing to get their hands wet or dirty or calloused.

Even when told to "respect authority," they will find ways to express their true feelings. To cite an example from history: The fifteenth-century spiritual awakening in Bohemia, fanned by the preaching of John Hus, was harshly squelched by the Vatican. Pope Gregory XII at one point declared a curse on Prague, closing not only the Bethlehem Chapel where Hus addressed standing-room-only crowds, but *all* the churches in the city of Prague—a terrible thing for faithful Catholics, who believed they had thus been cut off from the means of grace (the Mass).

> **All who represent Christ in the world are meant to be nothing more than humble servants.**

If you go to visit the Bethlehem Chapel today (beautifully restored), you will see two large paintings on the wall from that tense time. The two captions are telling. One shows Jesus on a donkey riding into Jerusalem, with crowds waving palm branches and singing hosannas. Its title: "This is the Lord." The other shows the pope riding on a bejeweled white horse, an entourage of cardinals in red capes behind him. Its title: "This is the servant."

Yes, indeed. All who represent Christ in the world are meant to be nothing more than humble servants. There is only one true Master.

Argentine pastor and author Juan Carlos Ortiz has written compellingly about the farm worker Jesus described who, after a hard day in the fields, came home and was required to fix the master's supper first before preparing his own. "So you too," said Jesus, "when you do all the things which are commanded you, say, 'We are unworthy slaves; we have done only that which we ought to have done'" (Luke 17:10 NASB).

Ortiz comments:

We are so upside down today that we give unworthy slaves a diploma that reads, "Reverend." Once I was in a meeting where someone was introduced with great fanfare. The organ played and the spotlights came on as someone announced, "And now, the great servant of God, — —."

If he was great, he was not a servant. And if he was a servant, he was not great. Servants are people who understand that they are worthy of nothing. They work eight hours and then come in and fix dinner for their Lord—and are refreshed and joyful when they see their Lord enjoying his meal.

May God help us to do with joy what servants in His Kingdom do.[13]

I can't say I've always ministered with the face of a servant. Among my struggles has been a penchant for flashy cars. In 1965 I purchased one of the first Mustangs ever produced. It was dark blue with a white vinyl top. Nice! When I started doing a lot of travel across the district in 1991, I decided to lease a Lincoln Town Car. (After all, part of my territory was Washington, DC.) The car was comfortable, and the color black made it look executive.

Admittedly, when I went to some of the rural churches, it felt a bit awkward to drive onto their gravel (or sometimes grassy) parking lots. But of course I was an executive leader and deserved this perk. No parishioner ever said anything. My wife, however, often expressed her disapproval.

One day back in Richmond, I was playing golf with a friend who had known me since my early days as a church planter. He looked at my black Lincoln and asked, "Is that your car?" This was God's way of speaking to me. As soon as the lease expired, I opted for a different model.

While there's nothing inherently wrong with driving a luxury car, for me it was an expression of *I've worked hard—I deserve this.* This kind of thing is subtle, but it happens. When you have access to the front of the line, can drive the luxury car, and sit at the head table, you can easily forget that power is not in having but in giving.

I do remember one day when I got it right, however. I had become friends with an eminent Presbyterian minister in Richmond, Dr. John Allen McLean. He had authored a couple of books and was highly respected across the city. Now eighty years old and retired, he did a favor for a friend and met with me. That began a mentoring relationship that was unique. He often said to me, "Bob, we Presbyterians taught people how to study the Bible. And you Pentecostals taught people how to experience it."

> **Jesus was always closing the gap between being the expected King-Messiah and being a servant.**

In the springtime, I would drive him around Richmond so he could enjoy the azaleas and dogwoods. He would share his life and ministry experience. As a young pastor, I drank from his well of knowledge.

Eventually they had to put Dr. McLean in the hospital, and we could see the end was drawing near. I went to visit him one day. "Dr. McLean," I said, "is there anything I can do for you?"

His reply was not what I was expecting. It was, in fact, almost straight out of John 13.

"Yes, Bob—I'd like for you to clip my toenails."

Well! Wasn't that the job of the nurses?

After a pause, I nodded and replied, "Sure . . . I'll do that. Let me go find a pair of clippers." I left the room briefly, then returned with the necessary equipment. I got a pan and a towel.

Dr. McLean sat up on the edge of the bed and put his feet down into the warm water, to soften them. Soon, I proceeded to clip ten toenails. Rather than feeling demeaned, I had tears running down my face. I whispered to myself, "I am grateful to be able to serve this man of God."

Jesus walked among ordinary people with feet that needed attention. He was always closing the gap between being the expected King-Messiah and being a servant. Some wanted to crown Him, but He kept placing Himself on ground level, tending to their practical needs for food, for companionship, for a gentle touch.

He expects the same of us. That's why I keep my toenail clipper near my Bible. It's a reminder for me.

# CHAPTER SIX

# Getting Practical

So how do we actually practice servant leadership on the busy Tuesdays and Thursdays and Sundays of our lives? The theory sounds noble as well as biblical. But what does it actually look like on the level where you and I live each week? Where does it find its "face"?

The key is to focus our attention on *people* and *mission (purpose)* as opposed to *systems*. Not that systems and structures are unimportant; they are. But they're not what Jesus died for. When the end comes, systems won't be going to heaven. Individual people, on the other hand, are what matter.

My friend Dick Foth, whom I mentioned earlier, says, "Jesus saw people as individuals, not as categories. He saw a lone woman at the well—not just a 'Samaritan.' He saw Nicodemus—not just a 'rich Pharisee.' He saw Zacchaeus—not just a 'tax collector.' And he adapted his style accordingly." He was "moved with compassion" (six different mentions in the gospels) as He zeroed in on individuals.

You can't really serve a category. Leaders are called to serve people, not issues. Some church leaders become so issue-oriented that they miss individuals along the way. I'm not saying that the issues are unimportant. But they have a way of making us more combative than service-oriented.

Servanthood means looking people in the eye instead of looking down from above. Granted, not everyone has been given equal talent. Not everyone can help the church move forward to the same degree. Not everyone can put the same size check in the offering plate. Some members of the body "seem to be weaker," even "unpresentable" (1 Cor. 12:22–23).

**Not everyone in the church is made for prominence, but everyone is significant.**

But in fact, Paul teaches us in this passage that "the parts that we think are less honorable we treat with special honor." That's servant leadership.

We have a tendency to confuse *prominence* and *significance*. Not everyone in the church is made for prominence, but everyone is significant. We must treat them that way.

When ordinary people drive into our parking lot and see that the closest space to the door has a "Reserved for Senior Pastor" sign . . . what does that communicate? It says that some people are more significant than others. Some people get privileges, while others don't. If that's the case, how about changing the sign to read "Reserved for Guests"? Even at the local grocery store, I've never seen a reserved parking place for the manager or owner.

If you come into the ministry with a sense of entitlement, people will smell it. If you neglect to thank them for what they do (because *of course* they should do those things as a good Christian), they will quickly sense who's on top of the pyramid here and who's holding up the bottom. But if you treat them the way you like to be treated, they will respect you . . . and follow you.

## Subtle Signals

People take notice of the little things that telegraph whether we are servant-minded or not. Our son, Rob, like a number of other young pastors across the country, has been experimenting with various ways to call for response at the end of his messages. Some sermons, as you know, lead the listener toward an honest conversation with God, i.e., prayer. Others, however, lead toward taking action out in the world. Rob borrowed the idea from someone to put together a chest filled with three-by-five cards naming specific acts of kindness, ways to serve in the coming week. One said, "Give away a favorite piece of clothing." Another said, "Pay the toll for the car behind you in line." Another said, "Pray for the mayor each day this week, and e-mail him about it." People could come forward and take a card at the end of the service . . . *including the pastoral staff!*

This kind of response is not just for "them." It's for us, too, who consider ourselves to be leaders. Part of our leadership is to demonstrate servanthood.

I heard about one pastor in Colorado who announced to his congregation that he would be absent from the pulpit on two Sunday mornings every year . . . in order to go work in the nursery. Somebody else would preach those mornings; he would be sitting on the floor holding babies. The smiles on moms' faces across the sanctuary were widespread that day.

Servant leadership in a church can be as simple as jumping in to help set up tables and chairs for an event . . . washing dishes at the end of a fellowship meal . . . shoveling snow from the sidewalks if needed. It's really about a mindset to serve versus a mindset that says, "My time is too valuable to get distracted with menial tasks."

E. Stanley Jones, pioneer Methodist evangelist to India, tells how things worked in the *ashrams* (week-long spiritual retreats) he founded back in the 1930s. Along with messages and prayer times, "our Christian ashrams include a daily period of manual labor as an integral part of our spiritual cultivation. This breaks down the barrier between those who normally work with their hands and those who do not. Big businessmen, doctors, professors, and bishops, when working alongside manual laborers, find a comradeship never known before. My job has been to go around with a bag and a sharp stick picking up litter."[14]

## Healing Old Wounds

Sometimes an act of serving can be a salve for long-standing hurts. In my area was a pastor named Wally Odom. He pastored a growing, thriving church in Virginia Beach that grew to a couple thousand. We were warm friends.

About the time I became district superintendent, some issues arose in his church. I had to respond to them. As a result, Wally and I got sideways—I can't remember all the details of what happened, but I do know it was painful for both of us. He ended up leaving the church and taking a group with him. We had to discipline him for that. Our long friendship was now estranged.

Eventually he and the pastor of the small congregation that remained in the building planned a merger that would make Wally the pastor. This action was against our counsel, and in fact, the building belonged to the denomination. It seemed the only way to resolve this deadlock was through the legal system.

One day I went to a meeting on the matter. Wally walked in and said, to my surprise, "I have looked at 1 Corinthians 6 (the passage on believers not suing each other). There is no way we should be settling this in court. You all keep the building; I'm not going to make an issue anymore. As a matter of fact, when I shared my insights about this passage this past Sunday, the congregation stood and applauded. They know what I'm saying at this meeting today."

Something broke in that moment. The relationship began to mend. And then he added, "And Bob, I'd like to have you come to our church and preach, so we can say to everyone that this matter is resolved."

I heartily agreed. The appointed date came around. The closer it got, however, I was perplexed about what to say. The Lord impressed me to preach about grace.

On Saturday evening, the Lord put a thought in my mind. What if I were to walk down to Wally during the sermon, take a towel, and dust off his shoes? Wow! That would be a lot to ask.

But the next day, I followed through. In the middle of my sermon, I said, "There is something I need to do today that's very important to help bring all of this to a resolution." I walked down, knelt in front of Wally and his wife, Gwen. I took out my towel and began to wipe his shoes.

People across the sanctuary began to weep. It's hard to describe the feeling of freedom that both Wally and I felt as we hugged each other.

Wally's credentials as an Assemblies of God minister were eventually restored. Sometime after that, he voluntarily withdrew because his ministry vision was taking him in a different direction. Nevertheless, at this past year's district council, we debuted a video about the reconciliation for everyone. E-mails came flooding in afterward. Younger pastors especially saluted the power of modeling servanthood.

**We need to give more spotlight in our churches to the ways in which people serve others.**

And every time I meet Wally Odom these days, he brings up the memory of that moment and how it freed him up in his ministry. Both of us say today that we'll never be the same after that experience.

What I did was just symbolic, I admit—but symbols and ceremony have always been important in the community of faith. Think about the Passover, with its meal of unleavened bread and its blood spatters on the doorposts. Think about the

Feast of Tabernacles, with people living in outdoor shelters for a week to evoke Israel's transient life in the wilderness. Think about Communion—the bread and the cup, which speak of Jesus' sacrifice for us. These things convey powerful messages.

## Examples to Showcase

We also need to give more spotlight in our churches to the ways in which people serve others. I know a lady who wasn't gifted to teach or sing—but she was a great cook. It so happened that another woman in the congregation named Camilla had a brain cancer. One day, she mentioned to her caregivers that she was hungry for some good Southern food—some collard greens and cornbread.

Nothing was said about this, but Helen, while at home, got an "impression" that she should make some food to take to Camilla. She just "happened" to fix the menu that was craved by Camilla—who was absolutely overwhelmed at this provision.

This is the kind of story that needs to be repeated in the public setting. It helps others catch the spirit of servanthood. It makes the theory practical.

Servants are people who have trained themselves to ask a certain kind of question in every situation or encounter. It is *not* "What do I feel like doing (or saying)?" It is *not* "What's the rule/policy/precedent on this?" It is *not* "How much is this going to cost?"

It is rather this kind of question: "What does he/she need? What's the gap to be filled here?" As we focus outward rather than inward, we position ourselves to render the most helpful service of all, in Jesus' name.

# CHAPTER SEVEN

# You Might Be a Servant If . . .

'm not a Jeff Foxworthy fan, but I want to draw a page from his 1993 "You Might Be a Redneck If . . . " piece, which topped the comedy album charts and sold more than three million copies. Using that paradigm, You Might Be a Servant If . . .

## 1. You walk into a room and say, "There you are!" rather than "Here I am."

Zacchaeus was surprised when Jesus called him by name and said, "I must stay at your house today." Admittedly, Zacchaeus' tax collection practice was not anywhere near the kingdom of God. But Jesus wanted to make a difference for him and the people he was fleecing.

The narrative gives no clue how long they visited or what they talked about. But the wrap-up announcement sent positive ripples through the community: "Look, Lord! Here and now I give half of my possessions to the poor, and if I have cheated anybody out of anything, I will pay back four times the amount" (Luke 19:8). It's amazing what can happen when we look for potential in people!

This concept resonated with all of us at a pastors' conference when Dary Northrop (Timberline Church, Fort Collins, Colorado) described how when some pastors of larger churches walk into a room, the vibrations almost scream, *"Here I am!"* Dary is pastor of an extremely large church, but he understands and practices authentic humility. When his church launched its campaign to finance a full-blown relocation, he geared up to take the first big offering. But in that context, he felt that God spoke to his heart, "I want you to give the first offering away to three other churches" that were also in building projects just then.

> **Letting others go first is not being a doormat; it is rather the doorway to a life of blessing.**

"I swallowed pretty hard at that," Dary admits. "We needed every dime we could raise ourselves. Our campaign target was massive compared to what these other three were seeking."

But he submitted to God's direction. He explained things to the congregation and, when the offering that day came to $33,000, he split it three ways and sent the money off to bless the other churches. In time, Timberline was able to fund its own expansion, too.

That's what I call a "There you are" type of leader.

## 2.  You let someone else go first.

Wanting to be first was a problem even among the disciples. Jesus rebuked them quickly. "Anyone who wants to be first must be the very last, and the servant of all" (Mark 9:35). I have a friend who says if we read and practice the red-letter parts of the Gospels (the direct quotes from Jesus), then everything else is a piece of cake. Well, maybe not, but I get the point.

All too often people rise to levels of success and begin to expect people to serve them. When those in higher positions continue to show humility by opening doors for others or standing so others can take the open seat, it models the spirit of Jesus. Letting others go first is not being a doormat; it is rather the doorway to a life of blessing.

Leaders are sometimes blind to their own actions. We serve people in our congregations and organizations—but neglect those closest to us, such as our spouse and family. Letting someone else go first should be practiced at home, so that those who know us best can believe in us the most in the public square.

## 3.  You don't care who gets the credit.

Ever wonder how speechwriters feel when the person giving the speech gets all the accolades? Or what about the one who writes the words to a song, but the performer enjoys the spotlight? And what about the lineman who makes the block that opens the hole for the running back to score a touchdown?

The disciples asked Jesus if they should put a stop to someone casting out demons because the person was not a part of their tribe (Mark 9:38). Were they saying it is better to leave a person in bondage if we can't claim the victory for our group?

Near the end of my tenure as pastor in Richmond, we brought a long-time friend of mine, Paul Wilson, from Florida to share in one of the Sunday services. Way back in the college dorm, we had given him the nickname "Bear" because of his size and his hairy body. Paul never did amass a lot of career credits to his resume, due to his limited eyesight and other physical challenges. In fact, he was declared legally blind and placed on disability status.

Yet for many years Paul had dedicated two hours every morning to pray for our church. The West End congregation gave Paul a standing ovation that day after he described how he had dreamed big dreams for people around the world from his prayer closet. We knew we were hearing from one of God's angels, even though I called him "Bear." He stood on that platform and wept as he said, "I'm getting to meet the people I've been praying for all these years!"

Soon he would go back home and resume getting up every day to continue his service of prayer. To this day, Paul Wilson doesn't care that other people are getting the public credits.

## 4. Giving makes you as happy as receiving.

The rich young man asked Jesus the right question, "What must I do to inherit eternal life?" Jesus gave him the right answer, "Go, sell everything you have and give to the poor, and you will have treasure in heaven. Then come, follow me." But the young man made a wrong decision, "He went away sad, because he had great wealth" (Mark 10:17–22).

**Hospitality is about making room for people to come into our space and feel welcome.**

Could it be that Jesus knew the young man wanted eternal life only so he could live forever with his riches? How sad! We know Jesus does not ask every person to give away all he owns to follow Him. But He does want us to love giving as much as receiving.

My grandmother helped frame this concept for me. She loved baking things for other people or taking vegetables from her garden to the church for the pastor, even when her only source of income was a small monthly check from the government. She always gave with a smile.

Since the greatest power we have as leaders is modeling, we must practice this principle no matter where we fit on the economic scale of life. It's one of the trademarks of servant leadership.

## 5. You practice hospitality rather than entertainment.

Hospitality is about making room for people to come into our space and feel *welcome*. Entertainment is about making room for people to come into our space to be *impressed*.

I know that Martha gets beat up in our sermons more than is necessary, but Jesus called her out for being "worried and upset about many things" (Luke 10:41). More than one person has said to me, "You preachers like to talk about Mary, but you can't run the church without Martha."

The point of the story, however, is that Mary made Jesus feel welcome in their home. Martha was distracted with all the preparations for the meal. Both of them were serving, but Mary had chosen the better way.

In our effort to make the venues of church, home, school, and office attractive, may we resist the temptation to put more attention on the ambience than on the people. After my last Sunday at the Richmond church where I had been pastor for twenty-two years, I took a late-night walk through the empty building. I strolled onto the platform and stood for a moment behind the pulpit. Looking at the beautiful sanctuary, I wondered why I didn't feel more emotion. Shouldn't I be choked up at this point of transition?

**The actions of servant-leaders end up on the pages of history.**

God spoke something into my spirit just then that took my breath away: *You can't cry, because the people are not here.* It hit me. His church is people not beautiful buildings made with hands.

## 6. You are recognized more for your serving than your title.

In 1982, Valley Forge Christian College outside Philadelphia was on life support financially. Dr. J. Robert Ashcroft, a prominent educator who was then seventy years old, agreed to be the president for a salary of one dollar per year.

On a beautiful windy autumn day, he pulled on some work clothes and began enthusiastically raking leaves near the front of the campus. As two men approached, they asked where the Administration Building was. He smiled and pointed them in the right direction.

Sometime later in the day, Dr. Ashcroft returned to his office wearing his normal suit and tie. You guessed it! The two men saw him and couldn't resist asking, "Aren't you the person we saw raking leaves?"

"Yes, I am," he replied. "That's one of the things I get to do these days as president."

Over the next couple of years Dr. Ashcroft (yes, he was the father of future Attorney General John Ashcroft) inspired others to join the effort to help keep the school open. Today the college is strong and vibrant, carrying out its mission "to prepare individuals for a life of service and leadership in the church and in the world."

Titles in an organization are placed on charts, desks, and doors. The actions of servant-leaders end up on the pages of history.

## 7. Your actions don't require a rear-view mirror.

As we know, Jesus never looked back and second-guessed His decision to wash the feet of the disciples, who would later hurt Him by betrayal, denial, and doubt. Learning to cope with disappointment and hurt inflicted by those who serve with us is simply part of Leadership 101.

My wife, Joan, loves the writings of Madeleine L'Engle. One of her favorite books is *A Live Coal in the Sea.* In this novel, the main character, Camilla, tries to explain to her granddaughter, Raffi, how she copes with hurt in her relationships. Camilla uses a quote that provides a life jacket when she's drowning in a sea of self-pity. "But all the wickedness in the world which man may do or think is no more to the mercy of God than a live coal dropped in the sea."[15]

If we want to become God's servant-leaders, we must embrace the truth that God's mercy absorbs human evil as though it were nothing more than a piece of glowing charcoal dropped into the ocean.

## 8. You understand when a towel has more power than a rod.

In his book *Jesus on Leadership,* C. Gene Wilkes says, "Jesus did not come to gain a place of power. He did not come to defeat his human enemies. He did not come to overthrow an unjust government. Jesus came to show us the heart of God. This is why on that night, the banner of the Kingdom was a towel stained with dirt."[16]

Jesus knew that Simon the Zealot no doubt expected Him to use force to set up His kingdom. I believe He also knew in advance that He would need to say to Peter, "Put your sword away!" (John 18:11).

The ministry of the towel is not suggesting there is no place for discipline or the exercise of strength by calling people to accountability. But God cares about whether we know when to use a towel rather than a rod to help fulfill our mission as leader. (If you don't believe it, ask Moses!)

## PART THREE

---

## The Face of a Steward

# CHAPTER EIGHT

# Performance Does Count

So far we've looked into two of the four faces of Jesus-style leadership:

1. The face of a shepherd (which has to do with our *calling*)
2. The face of a servant (which has to do with our *character*)

Now we turn to a third expression: the face of a steward, which has to do with our *competence*.

I can well imagine two opposite reactions at this point. One group of my readers is saying just now, "But the ministry is different from secular industry or government or finance. We're not trying to prove ourselves on some bottom line. To lead God's church is a high calling, as you already wrote in the first section of the book. We're 'dedicated' people . . . we're doing the best we can. What we do is so intangible. How could anyone put a gauge on it?"

The opposite group of readers is saying, "Well, it's about time! We were wondering, Bob, when you were going to get off the touchy-feely stuff and onto real skills. Enough mushiness already—let's bear down on strategic planning and productivity, with measurable outcomes. Christian leaders need to be held accountable!"

So that we're all on the same page, let me state that I'm using the term *competence* to mean the ability of an individual to do a job properly. For Christian leaders, competence is the combination of knowledge, skill, and behavior under the empowerment of the Holy Spirit.

What any of us is predisposed to think is not as important as what Jesus taught and modeled. From the Sermon on the Mount to His final words before the ascension, Jesus incarnated competence with authority. When He spoke, He never used a footnote or added a postscript. He was persuasive! Matthew 7:28–29 records that "when Jesus had finished saying these things, the crowds were amazed at his teaching, because he taught as one who had authority, and not as their teachers of the law."

His mandate to the disciples is the most strategic plan of the ages: "All authority in heaven and on earth has been given to me. Therefore go and make disciples of all nations, baptizing them in the name of the Father and of the Son and of the Holy Spirit, and teaching them to obey everything I have commanded you. And surely I am with you always, to the very end of the age" (Matt. 28:18–20).

Jesus is the one who told His followers to be ready and alert at all times, "because the Son of Man will come at an hour when you do not expect him" (Luke 12:40). Peter then asked for clarification, which led to this follow-up statement from Jesus: "Who then is the faithful and wise manager [KJV, NASB: "steward"], whom the master puts in charge of his servants to give them their food allowance at the proper time? It will be good for that servant whom the master finds doing so when he returns" (vv. 42–43).

**For Christian leaders, competence is the combination of knowledge, skill, and behavior under the empowerment of the Holy Spirit.**

He then went on to describe the slough-off manager, the fellow who thought he could kick back and take life easy while the master was away. Judgment came fast and stern. "From everyone who has been given much, much will be demanded; and from the one who has been entrusted with much, much more will be asked" (v. 48).

The apostle Paul echoed this obligation when he wrote concerning "those entrusted with the mysteries God has revealed. Now it is required that those who have been given a trust must prove faithful" (1 Cor. 4:1–2). He specifically and clearly applied this to local-church leaders in Titus 1:

> *An elder is a manager of God's household,* so he must live a blameless life. He must not be arrogant or quick-tempered; he must not be a heavy drinker, violent, or dishonest with money.

Rather, he must enjoy having guests in his home, and he must love what is good. He must live wisely and be just. He must live a devout and disciplined life.

TITUS 1:7–8 NLT, EMPHASIS ADDED

## Not Really Ours

Stewards or managers understand that the operation is not actually theirs. They are to run it well on behalf of the owner, which in the case of the church is God. This is not a "sole proprietorship" for the pastor or Christian leader.

Yes, I remember hearing people (even fellow ministers who should have known better) refer casually to the church I planted and led for twenty-two years as "Bob Rhoden's church." No, it wasn't! I was simply a steward trying to take good care of *God's* people. It was all His property, His enterprise.

In fact, any congregation is but a slice of "the church of God, which he bought with his own blood" (Acts 20:28). He paid a high price for this group of sheep. They're His, not ours. So the only question I should be asking at the end of a day is "Lord, did I take care of your flock today the way you wanted me to?"

Every April we credentialed ministers in the United States are reminded that the federal tax code classifies us as "self-employed." But we're not. We are working for an outside owner—and I don't mean the congregation, the district, or the denomination. I mean the "Chief Shepherd" (1 Pet. 5:4), whose authority far outstrips the IRS.

It's only reasonable that He would hold us to certain standards and expectations. Jesus dramatized this in multiple parables depicting

**The church . . . is not a "sole proprietorship" for the pastor or Christian leader.**

God as a landowner relating to His workforce. The most obvious is His story about the man soon to leave on an extended trip who gave out ten minas (traditionally, "pounds") in Luke 19:12–17 . . . or, in another iteration, various bags of gold (traditionally, "talents") in Matthew 25:14–30.

He "called his servants and entrusted his wealth to them . . . each according to his ability" (Matt. 25:14–15). Some got more gold than others, showing that we are not all equal—but we are all responsible. As you know, "after a long time the master of those servants returned and settled accounts with them" (v. 19).

The fellow who hadn't done anything with his boss's gold was really a sad case. The master ended up calling him not just incompetent but "you wicked, lazy servant!" (v. 26). Ouch. One commentary says that "wicked" here refers to the sin of omission, the failure to strive toward our God-given capacity.

Stewardship means that we give every effort to fulfill what God, the owner of the church, has in mind for us to do. He sets the agenda, and we do our best to follow it. We are in the employ of the One who made the universe to run with exquisite precision as well as amazing beauty. We are members of His staff and are expected to perform as such.

As you drive across the Great Plains, you may come to two small towns in two different states (Clarendon, Texas, and

Atwood, Kansas) with curiously named lodging establishments: the "It'll Do Motel." In other words, they're not the Hilton or the Hyatt, nor even a Holiday Inn. But if all you want is a bed for the night . . . "it'll do."

Stewards in God's kingdom are summoned to a higher standard. We work under the authority of the King of kings, to whom we owe our best. We "press on toward the goal to win the prize for God has called [us] heavenward in Christ Jesus" (Phil. 3:14).

## What Is God's Mission for Us?

Before we get down to particulars, we need to stop and focus on what God intends for us to do. The first step toward competence is to clarify the *mission* (or *purpose*). What is a church supposed to be, anyway? It's more than just a weekly event for which we have to get ready. How is the church put together? If we as stewards don't understand this, we'll never get the right things done.

Why is Google so successful in today's online environment? It has a simple eleven-word mission: "Organize the world's information and make it universally accessible and useful."[17] That's an extremely big undertaking! But it's clear what this company is about.

Jesus was equally succinct about His mission: "To seek and to save the lost" (Luke 19:10). He never let Himself get distracted from that.

Every leader has to come to terms with what is the purpose of his or her institution. At West End, we finally boiled it down to this: "Touching people for Christ." And how would we aspire to do this? Through five actions: worship, teaching, evangelism, prayer, and fellowship.

These were the things that would command our attention and energy as stewards. Other "good" activities would have to be left by the wayside.

Oswald Chambers once said, "It is easier to serve God without a [mission], easier to work for God without a call, because then you are not bothered by what God requires; common sense is your guide, veneered over with Christian sentiment. . . . But if once you receive a commission from Jesus Christ, the memory of what God wants will always come like a goad; and you will no longer be able to work for Him on the common-sense basis."[18]

Once the mission is clear, the next step is *not* to run out and get busy trying to fulfill it. It is rather to nail down our *core values*. What do we believe? What will we go to the mat for? What are the non-negotiables?

This list shouldn't be terribly long, or else we will lose track. Five to seven core values should be enough. Here's the list we distilled at West End. We said we would always be committed to:

- Relationships built on Christian love, trust, and transparency
- Integrity (truthfulness)
- Serving
- Cultural relevance
- Excellence

These things (and the mission as well) hold steady throughout time. They're permanent anchors for good stewardship. Language and style may change over time; the West End wording has now been updated to "We are committed to connecting people with Christ through worship, community, mission, and discipleship." But the essence remains the same.

*Vision,* on the other hand, is a different matter. It's what we see as a possibility in the present context that would fulfill our mission. For example, in pursuit of *"connecting people with Christ,"* we may see the need for a guest center that helps welcome people when they attend church on Sunday. Or we may decide to plant a new church, or to have multiple campuses of one church. Or we may develop a food and clothing center to help those in need. Or we may sponsor a monthly luncheon for seniors that includes a teaching component. We may even stretch outside our area to focus on an unreached people group in another country. The vision incarnates the mission, and the mission informs the vision.

> **The vision incarnates the mission, and the mission informs the vision.**

Vision needs to be updated on a regular basis. In Nehemiah's story of rebuilding the wall around Jerusalem, the full project took fifty-two days, and yet the people got discouraged halfway through the project and wanted to give up. From this story Pastor Rick Warren has developed what he calls the Nehemiah Principle: *"Vision and purpose must be restated every twenty-six days to keep the church moving in the right direction. In other words, make sure you communicate your purpose at least monthly.* It is amazing how quickly human beings—and churches—lose their sense of purpose."[19]

As a leader I cannot simply mention the vision once and hope everyone remembers it. I must state, restate, and clarify it over and over. It takes time for a congregation to take ownership of a vision. Otherwise, they just rent it. And we all know that tenants generally do not take care of property with the same care and attention as owners do.

Concurrent with rolling out the vision, we set some specific goals. We deduce that we will have to tackle certain activities in a certain order. If we do them successfully, we will have brought the vision to reality . . . and the mission will be advanced in a manner consistent with our core values.

*Vision* is synchronic. It changes from season to season. And obviously, so do the *goals* that measure it. *Mission* and *values,* on the other hand, are diachronic. They remain constant for long periods of time and are revised only as the environment demands.

The mission and core values of any church or organization may be similar to those of other churches and organizations that are like-minded. However, we must not simply copycat the visions and goals of others. If we do, we make the mistake of copying models rather than applying principles. For instance, several years ago many pastors tried to copy the vision of Tommy Barnett (Phoenix First Assembly of God), who used buses to bring people to church. It was a great vision, but not necessarily right for every church.

Seek God for His assignment tailored for you. In the words of Peter, "Each of you should use whatever gift you have received to serve others, as *faithful stewards of God's grace in its various forms* . . . so that in all things God may be praised through Jesus Christ" (1 Pet. 4:10–11, emphasis added).

# CHAPTER NINE

# Six Arenas to Manage

The call to be a competent steward/manager in God's work has many facets, of course. Here are six of the most important:

## Speaking on God's Behalf

To open our mouths (or to create text for any kind of display, print or electronic) as a steward of the Almighty is a serious responsibility. It calls for more diligence than the average conversation. There's a current popular phrase we hear or see on social media that goes, "I'm just sayin' . . . " To pick up a microphone or write a statement on God's behalf is a lot more than "just sayin'."

Jesus, our model, could claim in all seriousness, "The words I have spoken to you—they are full of the Spirit and life"

(John 6:63). The prophet Jeremiah scorched certain imposters who "speak visions from their own minds, not from the mouth of the Lord. . . . I did not send these prophets, yet they have run with their message; I did not speak to them, yet they have prophesied" (Jer. 23:16, 21). It is a fearsome thing to serve as God's spokesperson to His people.

Granted, we do have some influence on the verbiage. God lets us choose our own nouns and verbs—and we should do so with excellence. But the content must always be His.

**Good stewards treat both their message and their audience with respect.**

Our part in the preparation is a central element of stewardship. For those of us who enjoy verbal communication, it's easy to talk on and on without saying much. I appreciate the wisdom of one president of the United States in the late 1800s who, when asked to come speak at a certain occasion for just ten minutes, replied, "I'm sorry, but I would not have time to prepare adequately."

"Well, how long would it take?" the inquirer asked, incredulous. "It's only ten minutes."

"I would a need a week," the president replied.

"My goodness—what if you had to speak thirty minutes?"

"Well, that would take maybe an hour of preparation time," the president answered.

Now the person was totally confused. "What if you had to speak for two hours?" he said.

"Oh—in that case, I'm ready now!" the president answered with a smile.

I'm afraid I've listened to more than one sermon in my life from a preacher who was "ready now."

Good sermons do not need to be long, and a bad one definitely should not be! The number of preachers who can hold my attention for more than thirty minutes is limited. Some churches, I know, have developed a culture of expecting longer teaching sessions. However, these pastors are very gifted communicators. My experience is when they are *not* in the pulpit, and a staff pastor or even a guest speaker tries to match the one-hour performance, the sheep begin to squirm.

I learned from Chaplain Barry Black that good sermon preparation has three steps. I've taken the liberty to expand it to five:

1. Study until you're full
2. Think until you're clear
3. Pray until you're hot
4. Deliver with passion
5. —And land on time!

Good stewards treat both their message and their audience with respect. They make the most of the minutes allotted to them. They take into account the comprehension level of the listeners and choose words that will connect, so as never to hinder the transmission of God's truth.

In his book *Break-through,* Tom Rees tells about one of the most conscientious preachers of all time:

The Rev. John Wesley was a brilliant linguist. He corresponded with his family in Latin. He was a good Greek scholar, and well acquainted with the Hebrew tongue. Moreover, he spoke and wrote several modern languages fluently.

Yet, when he started preaching in English to the common people of his day, he discovered that his hearers just didn't understand his language, so Wesley had to learn yet another entirely new language—the language of the common man. Calling an illiterate servant girl into his study, he said:

"Now Mary, I want you to listen carefully to me. I am going to read one of my sermons to you, and each time I use a word or a phrase you do not fully understand, you are to stop me."

So, with the help of Mary he learned a new language, and went forth in the power of the Holy Spirit to offer Christ freely to the people in England in the tongue they spoke and understood.[20]

Boring people while proclaiming the good news is not only unwise—it may even be a sin. As Henry Ford noted, "Just because something has been said doesn't mean it has been communicated." Communication must be clear, concise, and correct.

If I am trying to communicate the most important news a person can hear, and if that person's destiny depends on his response, I must do it with my best skill under the anointing of the Holy Spirit.

# Serving as God's Diplomat

Another major part of stewardship is serving as the voice of reason and enlightenment to those who are in conflict with one another, or with you. This work is nobody's favorite, to be sure. But with any flock of sheep, it is essential.

The Prince of Peace pronounced a blessing upon those who would be "peacemakers, for they will be called children of God" (Matt. 5:9). The apostle Paul exhorted the Romans to "live in harmony with one another" and, a few verses later, "if it is possible, as far as it depends on you, live at peace with everyone" (Rom. 12:16, 18). He specifically instructed the young pastor Timothy, "Don't have anything to do with foolish and stupid arguments, because you know they produce quarrels. And the Lord's servant must not be quarrelsome but must be kind to everyone, able to teach, not resentful. Opponents must be gently instructed, in the hope that . . . they will come to their senses . . . " (2 Tim. 2:23–26).

> **A Christian leader ought always to be on the side of reconciliation, not aggravation.**

Granted, not every dispute can be mediated. I appreciate Paul's caveat about "if it is possible, as far as it depends on you." Sometimes the two sides absolutely will not bend. But a Christian leader ought always to be on the side of reconciliation, not aggravation.

Since conflict is endemic to human nature, we must learn to manage it in the church. It seems incredible that, immediately after settling the greatest conflict of the early church (Acts 15),

Paul and Barnabas split up over the dispute about Mark. But that is life in the ministry.

In writing to the church at Philippi, Paul pleaded with Euodia and Syntyche to agree with each in the Lord (Phil. 4:2). James asked, "What causes fights and quarrels among you?" (James 4:1). If we passionately point to the first-century church as though it were perfect, our view has been sanitized.

The primary issue for which Paul contended in his writing was unity in the church. He knew that a fractured church is dysfunctional. The church can only fulfill its mission when there is unity of spirit and purpose.

As a young pastor I faced a daunting situation that had huge potential for disunity in the church. Because of rapid growth, we had begun two morning services with education classes in between. It made for a long morning for all the ministry teams, plus it created overlapping parking issues in our limited space.

After some study, we proposed to the church board a schedule of two morning services with concurrent education classes for fifth grade and under. Education for sixth grade through adults would move to Wednesday night.

Two members of the board strongly objected, fearing that teens and adults wouldn't take the Wednesday slot as seriously. "People won't come out in the middle of the week for classes," they predicted. So we postponed any action for six months.

During that time I stumbled across two concepts about managing conflict. (1) Take time to build a strong consensus among key players, and (2) ask the opposition to agree to a one-year experiment, with the understanding that we can return to the way it was if the experiment is not working. (I'm amazed at what I've stumbled across at just the right time by talking with mentors, listening to audio materials, and reading. It reminds me that God really loves His church and wants to help us lead it.)

During the six months, we gained the support of the entire education staff and teachers as well as a number of parents. The board agreed to implement the idea as an experiment, although the two dissenters were not enthusiastic. But I have to say, the experiment worked, and as long as we had multiple services we followed the pattern. (Did I mention that Wednesday night attendance more than doubled in the next year? And that we even had to go to three Sunday morning services for a short time during construction expansion?) The experiment turned into a permanent solution.

Daniele Varè, an Italian ambassador to the imperial court of China in the 1920s, said once, "Diplomacy is the art of letting the other person have it your way." I like that! It is an art worth cultivating.

## Managing God's Time

The gift of hours and days is so commonplace that we can easily neglect their management. We take them as automatic and stop seeing them as a resource.

Leaders have to show initiative. Nobody should have to tell them to get out of bed and get moving. When I was a young pastor, I was good at sleeping in! It wasn't that I didn't work hard the rest of the day. But I thought it was all right to start slowly. After all, I'd probably be busy with people well into the evening.

One morning, a member of our church called around nine o'clock. I groggily cleared my throat and tried to sound normal.

"Did I wake you up?" she asked.

"Well, I was already awake . . . " I sputtered, which was only half the truth.

The Lord really spoke to me about that. *Bob,* He seemed to say, *some of your people had to be out late last night, too. But they're already up and at their jobs by eight o'clock this morning.* I vowed to change my habits immediately.

Another part of stewardship is being on time. It took me a while to grasp this, too. During my days as a youth pastor, I would saunter into meetings when I got around to it. My senior pastor, mentor, and father figure Ira Stanphill didn't like it.

One day as soon as I sat down at the conference table, he said, "Bob, do you believe the Bible?"

"Yes, sir!" I replied.

"Do you believe the part that says you're not supposed to steal?"

"Oh, yes!"

"Then stop stealing my time," he said, looking me straight in the eye. "Every time you're late, you're stealing time from me."

I was humiliated, of course. I've never forgotten the lesson of that moment.

Admittedly, there are many things that clamor for our time. If we're going to be diligent, we struggle to fit in everything that needs attention. We often talk about "prioritizing our schedule"—but I've found that we have to be more proactive than that; we have to schedule our priorities. We have to slot them into our days before other things take over.

The pastor of a growing church can be swallowed up by the urgent. In fact, some of us get addicted to urgency. On two different occasions I was hospitalized for what seemed to be a heart attack. But in fact, it turned out to be just stress. One day the physician came in, sat on the edge of my bed, and said, "Preacher, you just need to pace yourself better."

Not long after that, I had a dream one night. I was coming out of church—the last one out the door, as usual—and as I walked toward the parking lot, I saw a disheveled kid on the lawn. The closer I got, I realized he was smoking. Then I got even closer and smelled the distinct smell of marijuana.

I reprimanded him in my dream. "You shouldn't be doing that on the church lawn," I said. "You need to at least move along to somewhere else."

The young man then turned to look directly at me. "You don't recognize me, do you?" he said. "I'm your son, Rob."

I woke up crying. I knew I had to make some changes right away. I began blocking out time for my three children, who were then nine, seven, and five. I helped coach Rob's baseball team the next season. I made sure I was at school for the girls' concerts. My wife and I declared that Friday would be "Family Day," with time for such things as swimming at the Jewish Community Center where we had a membership, eating pizza followed by seeing a family-friendly movie, or taking a trip to one of Virginia's many historic and natural attractions such as Monticello or Luray Caverns.

Joan and I are happy to report that our three children, now grown and raising their own families, continue to serve the Lord.

## Delegating and Organizing

Closely related to the above topic is recognizing the fact that we as leaders will not be able to get everything done ourselves. We would like to, of course. We know the results we want, and we know how they ought to be produced. If we entrust someone else with this task or program, they'll probably just mess it up.

In his bestselling book *Good to Great,* Jim Collins talks about getting the right people on the bus and in the right seats.[21] To transfer that concept to a biblical model, we can turn to Exodus 18. Moses' father-in-law asked him, "Why do you alone sit as judge, while all these people stand around you from morning till evening?" Moses gave the answer of a conscientious pastor: "Because the people come to me to seek God's will" (v. 14).

If the average pastor trying to lead a couple hundred people feels overwhelmed, try thinking about Moses with two million people in his congregation. Have you ever felt like saying, "Something has to change around here?"

Moses' father-in-law dug even deeper. "What you are doing is not good," he declared. "You and the people will wear yourselves out. . . . You cannot handle it alone" (vv. 17–18).

One of the best things Moses did as a leader was to listen and act. What a lesson for us—to listen to good advice.

Moses selected capable men who walked with God and gave them a clear job description. The promised results saved his life and ministry. The father-in-law's prediction came true: "You will be able to stand the strain, and all these people will go home satisfied" (v. 23).

That is indeed getting the right people on the bus and in the right seats.

Jesus modeled a similar pattern. He selected twelve to work with Him (Luke 6:12–16) and then seventy-two more (Luke 10:1). The apostles followed the same pattern in Acts 6, when the first deacons were chosen to help in the daily distribution of food.

Building a church or company requires skillful delegating and organizing. We can delegate authority *but not responsibility*. So we give clear directions and write job descriptions, then set specific times for evaluation.

## Managing God's Money (at Church, at Home)

This is perhaps the most obvious arena for us to be good stewards. Whether we happen to like bookkeeping or hate it, the fact is that financial resources are not unlimited and must be carefully tended. A church seldom has "enough" funds at any time, but it will have even less if leaders do not manage with wisdom.

Jesus, after telling the story of the shrewd manager, said these words:

> Whoever can be trusted with very little can also be trusted with much, and whoever is dishonest with very little will also be dishonest with much. So if you have not been trustworthy in handling worldly wealth, who will trust you with true riches? And if you have not been trustworthy with someone else's property, who will give you property of your own?
>
> LUKE 16:10–12

Church funds are "someone else's property," namely, God's. They are not ours to manipulate. The parishioners understand this, the government understands this, and we had better understand it, too.

The early church got a stern lesson on this when Ananias and Sapphira lied about money that belonged to God (see Acts 5:1–11). It cost them their integrity and their lives.

The few pastors I know who have mishandled God's money did not begin with bad intentions. They started out "borrowing" small amounts, fully expecting to pay it back. However, no one else was notified about this clandestine borrowing . . . and trouble began to brew.

One person I'm thinking about was positioned to become the lead pastor of a strong church. Upon the current pastor's retirement, this man was elected to the top responsibility with more than 90 percent of the vote. But within just a few weeks, it was discovered that for a couple of years he had been taking church funds—more than $100,000—to acquire expensive home entertainment equipment and other such "toys" for his home. Once the facts were confirmed, he lost his position as lead pastor—and his ministerial credentials as well. The retired pastor, in shock, had to come back and guide the church up from its financial crisis.

> **Church funds are "someone else's property," namely, God's.**

Today, that church is strong again, but not without scars. It's a sad story that makes us pause and reflect . . .

Think about what it cost the pastor who stole the money.

Think about what it cost the older pastor, who had to delay his retirement.

Think about the people in the church, who lost much of their trust.

Think about the ripple effect of disappointment among ministry colleagues.

The church chose not to prosecute the man but to extend forgiveness. They showed him love . . . but trust will be a long time coming.

An extreme case, I admit. But even without malicious intent, many pastors don't know how to manage money—and aren't terribly concerned to learn. They seem to think that their life work is mainly about words, while numbers don't really matter that much. There is an old proverb that says, "Our income must exceed our outgo; otherwise our upkeep will be our downfall." Leaders have to focus on this important fact in order to avoid a crash down the road.

The second half of this is personal money management. Or maybe it should come first. If we cannot exemplify careful, responsible spending in our own homes, how can we hope to take care of a church budget ten or twenty times as large? And how will people be inspired to follow our example?

Yes, I know it can be hard to make ends meet on a pastor's salary. I remember a time in our early marriage when Joan and I said we just could not afford to pay our tithes. We believed in the biblical injunction, but . . . we said we would keep track on a piece of paper and try to catch up later, when our income was healthier. We practiced this for a number of months.

Then one day, we happened to be reading in an obscure corner of the Old Testament: "A tithe of everything from the land, whether grain from the soil or fruit from the trees, belongs to the Lord; it is holy to the Lord. Whoever would redeem any of their tithe must add a fifth of the value to it" (Lev. 27:30). The same rule applied earlier in the chapter to any dedicated house or animal the Israelite owner wished to reclaim. A 20 percent surcharge!

Joan and I looked at each other, looked at the bottom figure on the paper of unpaid tithes, calculated a 20 percent add-on—and said, "We need to stop this!" From that day to this, we have kept current with giving the Lord His portion. We've believed that part of stewardship is to keep our financial house in order, that we might be qualified to guide God's house as well.

## Managing Our Personal Walk with God

Finally, stewardship is about taking care to stay aligned with the One we serve. The steward holds to certain basic rhythms, as Jesus did: reading the Scripture, praying, giving. It is so easy to crave the big stage, the dramatic event. But underlying these must be a consistent personal walk with God.

This is more, and deeper, than just sermon preparation. C. S. Lewis wrote, "A man can't be always defending the truth; there must be a time for him to feed on it."[22] Before any topic is chosen, before any outline is drafted, we must humbly pray, Lord, what do you want to say to *me* through this Book?

We must constantly allow the Word to intersect with our life experience. If a leader's experience gets into the driver's seat, things can go badly astray. And of course, if we only read the Bible without connecting it to experience, we end up with a very dry life. The two must constantly intersect. In that, we thrive.

> **Stewardship is about taking care to stay aligned with the One we serve.**

There's a section in Leviticus 6 that I have come to love. (Okay, when did you ever read an author who cited Leviticus twice in one chapter? Strange, I know.) It tells how the priest was to go about handling the burnt offering. After its presentation to God . . .

> The priest shall then put on his linen clothes, with linen undergarments next to his body, and shall *remove the ashes* of the burnt offering that the fire has consumed on the altar and place them beside the altar. Then he is to take off these clothes and put on others, and carry the ashes outside the camp to a place that is ceremonially clean. The fire on the altar must be kept burning; it must not go out. Every morning the priest is to *add firewood* and arrange the burnt offering on the fire and burn the fat of the fellowship offerings on it. The fire must be kept burning on the altar continuously; it must not go out.
>
> LEV. 6:10–13, EMPHASIS ADDED

Two things were necessary to keep the fire burning:

One, "remove the ashes." When I was a kid growing up with my grandmother in a tiny shack in North Florida, we heated our three rooms with a fireplace. About once a week during the cold months she would say, "Bobby, it's time to take out the ashes." I'd get my shovel and scoop them out in order to let the next fire get a better flow of air.

Ashes are the residue of things that have been worthwhile in the past . . . but are now spent. Some traditions may have been good in days gone by, but now they're obsolete. They hinder the oxygen flow. We have to remove them. This is true of our personal lives as well as the institutions we manage.

Second, "add firewood." Bring in some new fuel for this morning's fire. Invite God's presence in a fresh way. I have a green recliner chair that has become the place where God and I meet in the morning. It's my Bethel. I'm big on designating a place and saying to God, "I promise to meet you there."

I know God can meet us anywhere anytime, but the discipline of setting a place that becomes sacred is important to me. I invite you to try it. God will fan into flame the fire of His presence in your life and ministry each day if you make time for Him.

Moses got a stark lesson along these lines at Kadesh, when the people were desperate for fresh water (Num. 20:1–13). He had faced this kind of challenge before, of course. So he did what he'd done last time. We can almost hear his thinking: *I know how to make water come out of a rock! You just hit it a couple of good whacks with a rod.*

God released the needed water, all right. But He also imposed a stern penalty on His steward: the loss of ever entering the Promised Land, which had been Moses' dream for decades. It's easy in ministry to think after a while, "Okay, I know how to handle this. I'm experienced by now." Not necessarily. God will give us fresh instructions at each juncture, if we take time to listen to Him.

## Manage Wherever You're Assigned

All these arenas of stewardship are present regardless of our location. Joseph had to prove himself with his father's flocks, then in Potiphar's house, and then in the prison before his big dreams ever came true. His brothers didn't show up to bow at his feet until he was thirty-nine years old. He had held faithful to his work for a long time ahead of that.

It's almost humorous how we make excuses about the environment in which God places us. When Joan and I first came to Richmond, some people said, "They'll never get a church started—especially a Pentecostal church—out there in the upscale West End, where all the doctors and lawyers live. It won't happen."

But after the church was up and growing, the comments turned to "Well, Bob Rhoden's got it made. He's out there in the West End, where all the money is!"

People seem to think the grass is always greener somewhere else. But being a steward means putting your head down and getting to work wherever you've been planted.

In the tiny mountain village of Rig, West Virginia, I met a truck driver named Brad Taylor who taught Sunday school. He wasn't the most sophisticated Bible expositor, to be sure. But he wanted to serve God. Every Sunday he would stand before his class and do the best he could.

In time, the pastor of that little church died. The congregation wanted Brad to succeed him. He wasn't at all sure about that. But my district staff and I worked with him, got him some training, arranged for him to be credentialed . . . and that church absolutely took off in growth. Brad Taylor was a good steward of what God had placed within him. He simply told God he would do the best he could with what had been put into his hands.

I'm not saying he would have been successful in a Washington, DC, church. But in his context—the setting God had for him—he was tremendously effective. He gave it his best, and God smiled upon his efforts.

God said once to a reluctant shepherd, "What is that in your hand?" (Exod. 4:2) Only a staff. God then put it to work, and a miracle broke out—the first of many for Moses.

The prophet Elisha repeated almost the same question to a desperate widow about to lose her two sons to the debt collector: "Tell me, what do you have in your house?" (2 Kings 4:2). Nothing but a small jar of olive oil, she answered. That became the source of another amazing miracle, as God provided an abundance for her.

What little we have is more than enough for God to use. When we willingly offer our small abilities and assets to Him, He makes us worthwhile stewards for His glory.

# PART FOUR

---

# The Face of a Seer

# CHAPTER TEN

# Do You See What God Sees?

O nce leaders prove themselves to be caring *shepherds,* willing *servants,* and competent *stewards* . . . their influence as visionary seers becomes timely and profound. This face of leadership was more frequent throughout the Old Testament than we realize. The word seer shows up some twenty-five times, referring by name to at least nine different people, starting with Samuel and running through Asaph (the psalmist) to Amos in the eighth century BC.

God's work always stands in need of those who can see what others miss:  opportunities, hazards, hidden talents, hidden motives, societal trends still in embryo, future attacks, coming waves of revival and renewal. Seers don't always come from a prominent heritage with a famous name; they may in fact arise from the shadows, like the obscure tribe of Issachar, which nevertheless produced "men who understood the times and knew what Israel should do" (1 Chron. 12:32). Their insight was invaluable.

Someone once asked the notable Helen Keller, "Is there anything worse than being blind?"

This marvelous woman replied, "Yes—to have sight but no vision."

Whenever God gives us a new level of ministry, it demands a new level of growth. Change is often unsettling—and this is when the ability to see is most crucial. God guided the people of Israel through the desert for years and years by a daytime cloud and a nighttime pillar of fire, providing manna each morning. But when they crossed the Jordan and entered the new land, the cloud evaporated. The pillar of fire disappeared. The manna stopped. It was a new season.

Joshua, the new leader, had to deal with a group of people who now needed to follow his *verbal* direction, and who would get their food from the land of Canaan. God was expecting His nation to change patterns. They had experienced His provision in certain ways up to now, but today would be different.

The temptation of the church is to want to go back and find the cloud again. It won't work. God instead is getting ready to knock down the walls of Jericho! He's working in new ways. The seer has to recognize this and help people see that God is still with us, even if it doesn't feel like yesterday.

James A. Belasco has written a fascinating management book titled *Teaching the Elephant to Dance.* He says that organizations are like elephants; they learn through conditioning. If you shackle a young elephant to a stake, he will grow up assuming he cannot move beyond a small circle. He may become very large and strong, but in his mind he will be limited: "I've always done it this way." So it is with institutions.

"Success ties you to the past," says Belasco. "The very factors that produced today's success often produce tomorrow's failures."[23]

The job of the seer is to envision what the elephant *could* do.

## Implementing God's Idea

Sometimes the new vision is a sovereign initiative from God—as in the case of Israel entering Canaan; this had long been His plan, and it was time to carry it out. The same can be said about the coming of the Messiah. God wanted to shake up the status quo, to introduce an entirely new voice into the religious landscape. Thus, Jesus became the archetypal change agent. He was repeatedly saying, "You have heard from the olden times . . . but I say to you . . . " He carried in His mind a far bigger picture of the future than the Pharisees, or even His own disciples, could imagine. He was a *seer*.

What is it that God might want to shake up in your current situation? What would He like you to *see* about the future that is unlike the past? My understanding of the brain is limited, I admit, but I'm aware of ongoing studies regarding the right and left hemispheres and how they relate to creativity and memory. As we get older, we tend to work more out of our memories than our creativity. When a church or organization functions more out of history than vision, it begins to die.

Trying to bring back yesterday will not produce a visionary tomorrow. We should bless the past and use it as a teaching tool to present a visionary future, an extension of the past. I can't prescribe the future of your church or organization—but I know it begins in the prayer closet of the seer. Nehemiah wept, mourned, fasted, and prayed before he arrived at Jerusalem to start rebuilding the walls. That part of leadership does not change with time or geography.

What is conceived in prayer results in the birth of holy initiatives. If it takes nine months for a natural pregnancy, it may take at least that long to develop a vision regarding your ministry.

I will always remember the first time I sat down at the superintendent's desk of the district office in my new role. I had been on the other side of this desk many times, as a local pastor in the district. In fact, I remembered a half-dozen trips up to this office in the Washington suburbs (a two-hour drive) when I had to face questioning by the presbytery about some innovation we were trying in Richmond. When my peers eventually elected me to this position, I was genuinely surprised. Didn't they know I was a maverick at heart?

**What is conceived in prayer results in the birth of holy initiatives.**

By the way, mavericks are not the same as rebels. Rebels defy the system and disregard spiritual authority. Mavericks challenge the system by pushing the boundaries of change, but they respect those in spiritual leadership. I guess I considered it part of my calling to be an "anointed maverick."

Now I looked down at the polished wood of this desk. I began opening the drawers. Everything had been cleaned out—except for one item. You will never guess what it was: a pair of handcuffs! I laughed and gasped all at the same time. Was this my new mission in life—to control the wild and crazy ministers across the Potomac District?

I knew the story behind the handcuffs. It had to do with the district camp up in the West Virginia mountains. A previous superintendent had, among other things, taken his turn as the night watchman there. He had carried the handcuffs as he made his rounds, in case an intruder needed to be restrained. I don't know that he ever had to use them.

But it got me to thinking long and hard about what my *real* mission was in this role. I spent one whole evening driving the Washington Beltway around the city, coming to terms with the core purpose for me and the staff. I finally saw during those several hours of windshield time that God wanted to shape the future of the Potomac District around a renewed mission and core values, with fresh vision and inspiring goals. In prayer (with eyes still open as I drove) I said, "I'm not sure I can do this. God, please give me your favor and anointing!" Now I was beginning to dial into the help I needed. I mentally asked God, "Where do we start? What should we keep? What should we eliminate?"

Shortly after that night, I had a very odd dream. I was in a funeral home, and I walked into a room where there was a corpse in a casket. As I approached the casket in my dream, the arms of the corpse began to move! Then the corpse sat up.

I awakened wondering what it all meant. When I began sharing the strange dream, someone said, "I believe the moving arms stand for hard work. And the person sitting up is a signal of renewed life."

Thereafter, our district leadership team began the hard work of codifying our purpose and core values, with a renewed vision of church planting. Within a couple of years, various local churches had planted seventeen new churches, and a number of existing churches were experiencing new life in the Spirit and revival.

We also started a mentoring initiative for younger ministers. Dick Foth and I met with them four times a year for a full day. We shared our history, what we had learned from our successes and failures in ministry, our marriage journey (with our spouses present for that session, which was actually an overnight retreat). In our final session of the year, we opened it up for questions about areas we had not yet covered, then prayed for each person in the group. It has been a joy to see many of those young ministers take up positions of strong influence in the local church and beyond.

## Needed: New Thermostats

This same kind of examination must take place at the local-church level. The point for a pastor is not simply to keep a lid on things, to maintain the status quo, to keep the wheels greased. A leader is to be a thermostat, not a thermometer. Leaders seek to know what is in God's heart, then set the tone of the discussion. This calls for boldness, for being secure in one's calling. But that's the essence of leadership, which I define as *courage in action.*

This may sound theoretical—but in fact, it gets specific as you live it out. I know a pastor who saw the need to add 100 parking spaces to the church's lot. Of course, it's not easy to raise money for asphalt. But he and his team weren't doing this just to provide business for the paving company. They linked the project to the church's mission, which was to provide access to the gospel of Jesus Christ. Out of this came their slogan, "Asphalt Gives Access." The congregation caught the larger point, and the necessary money was raised.

> **A leader is to be a thermostat, not a thermometer.**

If a leader does *not* make this kind of connection, people can assume it's just a matter of personal preference or ambition. If they think you're proposing a change just because you want to, they'll wonder why you're pushing this. There has to be a theological undergirding for the change, for the outlay of money.

I've spoken earlier about my days as a youth pastor in Lancaster, Pennsylvania. It was a traditional-style building, with the choir loft at the center back of the platform, and two benches directly in front for ministerial seating. The senior pastor (Ira Stanphill), however, loved music and wanted to be able to see the choir as they sang. So one day he moved the benches to an angle.

Would you believe that some people found this upsetting? It wasn't the way the church had always been. But they tolerated it, saying little; after all, they respected their pastor.

Then came his resignation. He preached his last sermon on a Sunday night, and . . . trust me, his car was not even outside the city limits on Monday morning before a crew of men were unbolting those two benches and putting them back straight! The change had not been tied to any larger purpose or value.

## Cultural Winds

Other changes come about as the seer perceives a shift in the cultural winds. Today is not like the 1970s or the 1980s or even the 1990s. And even if they were, individual people are not in the same season of life as they were back in those decades. They've traversed from being young singles to newly married to busy parents to . . . the fact is, nobody stands still. Boomers are less loyal to church traditions than their predecessors were. They care little about the name on the sign out front. They care deeply, however, about what connections they're making with other people.

Generation X and Generation Y are different yet again. They're less keyed to propositions and more keyed to narrative (that's why they watch so many movies). They don't worry about efficiency and pragmatic solutions; they just want to be "authentic" and "real," even "raw."

On top of this, our society is subject to constant cross-pollination as people move geographically. They bring values and ideas from Dallas to Minneapolis, or vice versa, that stir the pot. Plus, we have internationals arriving all the time.

All of these changes are significant to those who try to lead. It's important to keep current with the shifting cultural winds—so long as they do not become our master. We can turn into full-time armchair sociologists if we're not careful. If we become obsessed with chasing whatever is "hot" at the moment, we'll lose our tie to the One who called us to serve *His* interests. He is the One who truly knows what's going on and how He wants us to relate to the present milieu.

We sometimes think we're in a unique, never-seen-before environment. But stop and think a minute about the world of the first century. The crowd that gathered downstairs from the Upper Room on the Day of Pentecost spoke more than a dozen languages. Peter stood up and had to address everyone from local Jews to North Africans to Mesopotamians. If you analyze his message, he spent a good 75 percent of the time just talking about Jesus—which might be a worthy model for us in today's multicultural world. Peter rose above style, subculture, and personal preference. No wonder "about three thousand were added to their number that day" (Acts 2:41).

We know from reading both Acts and the Epistles that the Jew-Gentile differences were huge in the early church. These two cultures were not compatible; some Jewish believers didn't think Gentiles even belonged inside the church, under any terms. It took a seer like James to speak up in the Jerusalem Council and quote a prophecy from Amos 9, followed by, "It is my judgment, therefore, that we should not make it difficult for the Gentiles who are turning to God" (Acts 15:19). It took another seer named Paul to write that "Christ . . . has made the two groups one and has destroyed the barrier, the dividing wall of hostility. . . . His purpose was to create in himself one new humanity out of the two, thus making peace, and in one body to reconcile both of them to God through the cross, by which he put to death their hostility" (Eph. 2:13–16).

These were not popular sentiments in many quarters. But they were right.

In our time, we who aspire to build God's church are sailing into a stiff societal headwind called "niche." More and more people today hold stronger and stronger opinions about what they like, and don't like. If the subject is restaurants, the menu choices are Italian, Chinese, Mexican, Thai, Middle Eastern, Greek, and a dozen other specialties. If the subject is radio, you've got country stations, rock stations, talk-news stations (some "liberal," others "conservative"), adult-contemporary stations, classical stations . . . the list goes on and on. Choice is king these days.

And here's the church of Jesus Christ trying to be a *family,* which by its very nature means cross-niche and heterogeneous.

> **The family of God desperately needs wise, perceptive leadership to bring diverse people together.**

Look at any family around the Thanksgiving table; there may be fourteen-year-olds and thirty-four-year-olds and fifty-four-year-olds and maybe even seventy-four-year-olds. There are males and females. Some of them may live in metropolitan areas, while others are from small towns. Each person has to flex for the others. That's the nature of a family.

Close by the campus of Virginia Commonwealth University in downtown Richmond sits a church called, fittingly, Commonwealth Chapel. Its congregation of some 500 attendees is, as you might imagine, young and urbane . . . the Starbucks crowd.

But there's also a dear saint affectionately known by the rest as Sister Chappell, now in her eighties. She's been there since the days long ago when the church was called Bethel Assembly of God. At this stage of life, she's not going anywhere else! And the young people honor her. I've been in the Tuesday night prayer gathering and have seen her shuffle down the aisle in her matronly flowered dress and tennis shoes, approach the microphone and start "testifying," maybe even sing a bit of an old-time song—and the jeans-and-sweatshirt crowd breaks out in applause. She's not a category to them, an "old lady" from the dusty past. She's a person, a sister (well, maybe an aunt) in Christ. It's a beautiful thing to watch.

The family of God desperately needs wise, perceptive leadership to bring diverse people together under the common rule of Christ. As Dr. Harvey Herman, a specialist in campus ministry, puts it, we must proclaim "mystery in an age of information, hope in an era of skepticism, confidence in a time of doubt, and truth in a climate of relativism." That is the role of a seer!

# CHAPTER ELEVEN

# Advancing the Bigger Picture

The need for vision, for "farsightedness," comes up in multiple aspects of church life. Here are several of them:

## New Populations (Faraway, but Also Nearby)

When we think about mission work, we naturally affirm that God wants people in Bolivia and Botswana and Bulgaria to know about His saving love and grace, and so we should move that cause forward. But perhaps just as critical is that God wants to stretch *us,* to lift our eyes above our local American setting and make us truly Kingdom-minded.

Paul had the right perspective when he wrote, "It has always been my ambition to preach the gospel where Christ was not known. . . . As it is written, 'Those who were not told about him will see, and those who have not heard will understand'" (Rom. 15:20–21). He was what we call today a "world Christian."

I remember when West End was in the throes of its difficult building program, mentioned earlier. Our eyes were riveted on the construction costs and whether we would be able to meet them. Rumblings among the people grew louder.

One morning Associate Pastor John Hershman approached me with what he called "a crazy idea that might be God's way of helping us out of this mess." What if we were to lift our attention off our needs and reach out to a congregation in even greater need—say, some church in a Third-World country? We could take a team of people from our church and construct a building for them.

> **The leader who is a true *seer*, however, takes stock of who in the community is *not* receiving the gospel.**

It was so outlandish that it actually caught fire among the leadership and the congregation. We contacted Mike Hines, a missionary evangelist, who excitedly told us about two towns in the Dominican Republic where churches had recently been birthed as a result of preaching crusades. Could our vision be doubled?

The outcome of this discussion was that West End allocated $20,000 to build two buildings for two congregations we had never met. Twenty of our members even paid their own airfares to erect the structures. It was the beginning of a miracle. Over the next two years, all the money we needed back home to pay our past-due bills (about $200,000) was generously and joyfully given.

Is it a coincidence that we gave a tithe before God supplied our need? I don't think so. Neither was it a case of magic. Our experience simply intersected with what the apostle Paul wrote long ago: "Whoever sows sparingly will also reap sparingly, and whoever sows generously will also reap generously" (2 Cor. 9:6). We reaped not only financially but also in participation, as our attendance grew by 10 percent during those same two years.

But the need for vision that will touch new populations is not always across the water. Sometimes it's right in our own back yard. When the disciples were preoccupied in Sychar with figuring out how to arrange lunch, Jesus said, "I tell you, open your eyes and look at the fields! They are ripe for harvest" (John 4:35). He couldn't let them stay focused on just their own stomachs, or their own ethnic group. These Samaritans needed the Good News, too.

Churches have a natural tendency to focus on "our own kind." Birds of a feather flock together. The leader who is a true *seer,* however, takes stock of who in the community is *not* receiving the gospel. Who's being left out? Who is being underserved?

Is it college students? Is it migrant workers? Is it people of color? Is it those who don't speak English, or don't speak it well? Is it the incarcerated? Is it the military community, especially the dependents left home during long deployments?

In 1992 Frank and Lisa Potter came to a small church in Farmville, Virginia, a town of some 7,000 an hour or so west of Richmond. What they didn't know about Farmville and surrounding Prince Edward County was its egregious history.

Back in 1959, after the federal government had ordered school desegregation, Prince Edward County had simply put its foot down; it would stop funding public schools altogether. The white students were quickly enrolled in private academies set up in churches, while the African-American students basically had no place to attend school. This went on for the next five years, cementing a racial divide that was still very pronounced when Frank and Lisa arrived decades later.

Frank knew he was called by God to minister to everyone, not just the white folks in his church. So he began to pray and make friends with any African-American whom God put in his path. If white people glared at him, he simply gave a wave of the hand and smiled.

He didn't see quick results. But he kept going. It was not until thirteen years later that a short, elderly black man showed up one Sunday morning to hear Frank preach. His face was weathered from the wear and tear of hard years working as a farmhand; he wore sneakers, jeans, and a T-shirt as he slid into a back-row seat near a wall. Only four-feet-ten in height, his name (it was later learned) was simply "Little Joe."

At the end of the message that day, Pastor Frank gave a traditional altar call. The first hand to go up was Little Joe's. He promptly walked up to the altar and gave his heart to Christ. In talking afterwards, more facts came out: He had heard about this church and its pastor in conversations around town . . . he was seventy years old . . . he was the father of twelve children . . . his wife had chronic health issues that needed prayer.

The next Sunday, Little Joe was back in church—wearing a three-piece suit and gleaming dress shoes. He didn't sit in the back this time; he made his way clear to the front to sit alongside his new friend Pastor Frank. As church members stared at the back of his bald head, the symbolism was obvious: By welcoming Little Joe, the pastor was saying that this was a case of God at work, and no one should oppose what God was doing.

On the third Sunday, Little Joe handed a small vial of oil to Pastor Frank and asked him to pray over it each day the coming week. "Then I want to anoint my whole family," he explained. "I want them to find the joy I've found." Pastor Frank smiled and said he would be glad to consecrate the oil for such a high purpose.

But Little Joe's dream ran into tragedy that very Tuesday night—when he was killed in an automobile accident. This brand-new child of God was suddenly elevated to his eternal home.

The devastated family wanted Frank Potter to conduct the funeral. Taking the vial of oil to the pulpit that day, Pastor Frank preached and then announced, "I'm going to do what Little Joe had in mind for all of his family. For all who are willing, I'd like to anoint you with this oil as a sign of God's love and care for each of you."

The funeral ended up running for three hours, as black family members in a white church sang, danced, and knelt at the altar. It was the beginning of the "color wall" coming down in that church. Today, about 700 people (85 percent white, 15 percent African-American) worship together—including three of Little Joe's children and their families. His grandkids are in the children and youth programs of the church.

This congregation is now perhaps the largest church in Prince Edward County. There is still a lot of work to be done, of course. But one seer—Frank Potter—is making a difference in Farmville by pursuing the bigger picture of what God has in mind.

## Facilities

It obviously takes vision and courage to see when a larger facility is needed to accommodate the work of God. Notice the word *needed*. I'm not talking about building a bigger place just to make us feel proud of ourselves. No doubt many an American church building project has had more to do with ego enhancement than with Kingdom advancement.

But if the need is genuine, if the sanctuary is crowded, if young people's programs are being squeezed, if visitors are frustrated by lack of parking, then the leader with vision says, "We need to do something about this."

Drawing up plans is exciting. Figuring out a plausible budget gets a little more complicated. And then raising that budget requires even more steadfastness. In fact, all along the way there will be situations—even surprises—that call for skillful handling.

In 1986 our church was continuing to outgrow its facilities. We had moved Sunday services to a larger activities building near the back of our property, leaving the small octagonal chapel with cedar shake shingle roof for smaller meetings. The top of the chapel's steeple was crowned with a cross that had a lightning rod from the historic St. John's Church downtown—the building where Founding Father Patrick Henry gave his epic "Give me liberty, or give me death!" speech back in 1775. During the renovation of St. John's, their electrical contractor (who also happened to be working on our building) had asked if we wanted the lightning rod. We had said yes, of course.

**No doubt many an American church building project has had more to do with ego enhancement than with Kingdom advancement.**

Now as we considered our lack of available space to expand further, the president of a local synagogue called and asked if we could talk about their congregation purchasing our entire campus. He and I quickly agreed on a price and terms to take to our respective governing bodies. They were willing to put down a $50,000 nonrefundable deposit. He also asked if they could begin sharing the chapel as soon as we signed an agreement, since their Friday night/Saturday morning rhythm would mesh well with our Sunday/Wednesday schedule.

There was just one problem. They could not consecrate a building for synagogue use, he explained, if it had a cross anywhere in or on it. Would we be willing to remove the cross as part of the agreement?

I said we would give that some thought.

It took us a full three months to face and answer the questions that began popping up. Would we be compromising our public testimony that we had upheld for fourteen years on this campus? What would people think of a church taking down a cross—especially on such a busy avenue? What would this say to our children—that the cross of Christ didn't really matter that much to us?

We made a list of people who might have sentimental attachments to the cross because they were present on the day it was installed, had taken a picture at some particular time of day with a beautiful sky background, or had proudly told a friend that it came from St. John's. Those people and others received individual attention from one of the leaders—an invitation to lunch or a phone call, or both.

We held a meeting to focus solely on the cross issue. About 150 people showed up. We reminded ourselves that although symbolism is important, our faith is not tied to a symbol on top of a building. We reviewed the teaching of Scripture that "the Most High does not live in houses made by human hands" (Acts 7:48). We let people express their feelings both pro and con. We talked about the possibility of taking the historic cross with us to our new property down the road.

When we took a straw poll that night, only a half dozen people opposed the removal, and even they made it clear they still favored selling the property. Folks went home feeling a sense of ownership in the discussion.

The formal business meeting finally came around. The vote to sell to the synagogue—including the cross removal as they had requested—was unanimous. To my knowledge, no one felt railroaded. We could move forward in unity. In the days that followed, people began to turn from their stance of "Why would we want to do this?" toward "So when is the cross actually coming down? I want to be there to watch!" The day I announced the date of removal (with the promise to take it with us to the new building as a reminder of God's grace and blessing upon us at the current site), the congregation broke out in applause. We had maintained our peace without compromising our message.

And several months later, would you believe the Jewish congregation asked if I would speak at one of their Friday services? I agreed and immediately began asking God for guidance. I spoke that evening on the compound names of God in the Old Testament (e.g., Jehovah-shammah, Jehovah-rapha, etc.) and concluded by saying that while for them the story ends there, we believe the names are all fulfilled in Jesus, and that's the message we proclaim. I concluded with a prayer.

At the reception that followed downstairs, one of the members jokingly asked if I wanted to consider becoming their rabbi. Wow—I would never have been given the opportunity to share with them if we had not taken the cross down a few months before vacating the building.

Today the historic cross still rises into the sky atop the bell tower of the new West End Assembly of God. The church is as committed to the message of Calvary as it ever was. And its cohesion remains intact.

My point is that we have to recognize what is a "wineskin" for the truth and what is the actual truth. The skillful change agent—the seer—must be able to adjust methods and styles and traditions without changing the message. Many formats in the postmodern era today need to be different from what they were in the modern era when we were growing up. But we cannot forfeit the essence of what the Bible teaches, the bedrock theology of our faith. That is not negotiable.

# Music Styles

Another area of church life that is taxing many current congregations' ability to "be family" together is worship repertoire and style. Many pastors struggle today to accommodate strong opinions on this subject. Others have simply opted to go with one genre (usually pop-rock) and dismiss all others as unimportant or impractical.

It may be helpful to remind ourselves that this is not necessarily a new challenge. Gordon MacDonald says, "There have been four times in American church life when people split over music and forms of worship"[24]—the late 1600s (Isaac Watts and the introduction of hymns that didn't originate with the Psalms), the mid-1800s (gospel songs, e.g., Fanny Crosby and others), the 1920s (the simple choruses of Paul Rader, etc.), and our current period (contemporary gospel music).

Music is an art form, and people have been fussing about their artistic preferences for a long time. Behold the minutes of a 1736 business meeting at First Congregational Church, Windsor, Connecticut, as recorded by a somewhat irritated secretary:

> Society meeting, Capt. Pelatiah Allyn, Moderator. The business of the meeting proceeded in the following manner:
>
> The Moderator proposed consideration of what should be done respecting that part of publick Worship called Singing, whether in their Publick meetings on Sabbath day they would sing the way Deacon

Marshall usually sung in his lifetime, commonly called the "Old Way" *[by ear, imitating a leader one line at a time]* or whether they would sing the way taught by Mr. Beal, commonly called "Singing by Rule" *[using written notes]*. And when the Society had discoursed the matter, the Moderator proposed to vote. . . .

But when the vote was passed, there being many voters, it was difficult to take the exact number of votes in order to determine on which side the major vote was; whereupon the Moderator ordered all the voters to go out of the seats and stand in the alleys [*aisles*], and then those that were for Deacon Marshall's way should go into the men's seats, and those that were for Mr. Beal's way should go into the women's seats. . . .

The Moderator asked me how many there was for Deacon Marshall's way. I answered 42, and he said there were 63 or 64, and then we both counted again and agreed the number being 43. . . .

Then the Moderator proceeded and desired that those who were for singing in Publick the way that Mr. Beal taught would draw out of their seats and pass out of the door and be counted. They replied that they were ready to show their minds in any proper way where they were, if they might be directed thereto, but would not go out the door to do the same, and desired that they might be led to a vote where they were, and they were ready to show their minds—which the Moderator refused to do, and thereupon declared that it was voted that Deacon Marshall's way of singing, called the "Old Way," should be sung in Publick for the future, and ordered me to record the same, which I refused to do under the circumstances thereof and have recorded the facts and proceedings. [25]

What a sweet gathering of the brothers and sisters in Christ! The moderator was obviously more concerned to rig the voting his way than to keep the unity of the fellowship.

A pastor must say repeatedly, "I am the shepherd of *all* the sheep. Not just the noisy ones." Part of discipleship is to model and then teach mutual respect for those who don't share our style preferences. We may not love a particular song, but we can still love those who do find it useful for drawing close to God.

This whole issue in the modern church is, at its foundation, not so much about music style as it is about ecclesiology. It's about our grasp of what a church is and how we are to care for one another.

> **Conflict can arise if methods get turned into values.**

Everyone has a legitimate right to preserve memories of the past. And music often puts us in touch with those memories. Personally speaking, when I sing the hymn "It Is Well with My Soul" or "Like a River Glorious," I'm transported back to being a seventeen-year-old in the Toccoa Falls Bible College chapel, where I was thinking, *Wow—what a song!* I'd never heard these classics before.

Now of course, those songs might mean nothing to you. But the wise seer doesn't try to rob people of their memories of walking with God. He or she seeks to provide a way to stay in touch with that heritage. Meanwhile, new memories are being built all the time among others in the fellowship, and they too need ways to cherish those.

I know of a church that, like many today, has opted to have several different formats running simultaneously on Sunday morning. One is more classical, with full choir and orchestra, accompanied by keyboard instruments. Another is guitar-driven, with newer repertoire. Both services are growing, and they share the same preaching.

But once a quarter, they all come together on a Friday night for what they call a "One Generation" service. They mix up the songs, seeking to build respect and appreciation across age and style lines. Not everybody in every row "likes" everything, but they own the concept of being one family together. They seek to show their love for one another.

We would never think of robbing a fellow Christian of his money. Why would we rob him of his memories?

I honestly believe that you can tell more about what a church believes by how they manage differences than by reading their doctrinal statement.

## Youth Innovations

Young people instinctively define themselves by pushing the envelope, by being different from their forebears, whether in hairstyle, music, clothing, or jargon. This push for self-distinction shows up in church life, obviously. How leaders handle this says a great deal about their ability to see the bigger picture.

Conflict can arise if *methods* get turned into *values*. A case in point: One congregation was convinced that respect for God's house precluded eating in the church building. After all, this was sacred space, not to be desecrated with food and drink. Hadn't Jesus thrown the merchandisers out of the Temple to make that very point?

But the youth group had a bright idea for raising money to give to a missions project. They wanted to make and sell ham sandwiches ahead of the Wednesday night activities. That way people could come straight from work, buy a quick bite to eat, and get on to their meetings.

The pastor and board of deacons gave their approval. But a number of people disagreed. They felt the leaders were letting down a standard that had stood for many years. Maybe their leaders weren't worthy of their position after all . . .

I'm sorry to report that this festered into such a conflict that the church actually split! How sad, and how unnecessary. (I could understand a synagogue splitting over ham sandwiches, but a Protestant church?)

I faced my own dicey situation as superintendent when, in the mid-1990s, the Youth Department began pressing me for a swimming pool at the district camp. "We could get so many more kids to come to camp if it had a pool," they said. Up to that point, the only option was to transport campers a mile away to the Potomac River.

I knew this subject had been taboo in our conservative fellowship for a long time, due to issues of swimsuit modesty and "mixed bathing." Several leaders told me that although the pool was a good idea, it wouldn't sell at the grass roots. My wife, who had been raised in this district from the time she was a little girl, filled me in on some of the history.

So we started the discussion cautiously. We held some small focus groups to discuss "what if?" We drafted policies to take care of the modesty issue. The most interesting event was when I drove up to the camp to meet with all the retirees who had leased lots and built there.

"Please understand," I began, "that we do not want to do anything to offend you. We are sincerely seeking to know the wise decision in this matter. And I know you love the young people of this district as much as anyone. You care about them having genuine encounters with God."

The conversation proceeded in a calm and respectful manner. People got to speak their minds on the subject. The classic moment came when dear Sister Kibbe, probably in her eighties, stood up and said, "You put in that pool, Brother Rhoden, and I'll be the first one to jump in!" The whole place howled, of course.

The project was a success. We raised the money, and the pool is there today, with a gym right beside it. Kids are coming not only in the summer but during school breaks as well to deepen their walk with the Lord.

Sometimes managing change is simply a process of building a consensus in advance. The seer doesn't always have to come thundering off the mountain with a unilateral word of direction. Though he may know on the inside what God wants, it's helpful to bring others gradually to the same understanding.

Being a seer doesn't give anyone permission to overpromise, twist arms, manipulate, or exaggerate. In a certain church I saw one man's ministry come to an early end in less than three years, because the board and staff felt they could not defend some of the things he said and did. I was there the day he resigned; it was difficult, both for the congregation and for the minister. His spin on information was intended to create a positive perception of how things were going, but instead it had come across to the leadership as being untruthful.

God calls us to lead not only with boldness but also with integrity and sensitivity.

## Potential Leaders for the Future

One of the most important—but often neglected—things for a seer to notice is the calling of God on a person's life for significant ministry. It may be a gangly teenager; it may be a twenty-something already in the early stages of a career; it may be a soldier just finishing active duty; it may be a married couple approaching early retirement. Jesus told His disciples to "ask the Lord of the harvest, therefore, to send out workers into his harvest field" (Matt. 9:38). Part of the prayer needs to be for our own eyes to see those individuals God wants to develop.

Our influence on them may take any number of different shapes. In casual conversation we can say, "Have you ever thought about going into some kind of ministry work? If so, I could help you prepare . . . " The actual preparation can range from one-to-one appointments to online courses to enrollment in a full ministry training college. Paired with this is the chance to serve at the local-church level, to get practical experience in whatever specialty fits the person's gifts.

I once had the privilege of spending a day with Dr. Howard Hendricks, beloved professor at Dallas Theological Seminary. I had appreciated his writings over the years, and it was a joy to actually meet him. By this time I was a district superintendent, and I asked him, "If you were in my place, what would you say to ministers?"

Without hesitation, he answered, "I would say, 'Your potential is my mission.'"

When God looks at each of us, He says the same thing. He believed in us so much that He sent His Son to give His life for us. He sent the Holy Spirit to live within us. He is all about developing our potential.

Don't let yourself think you're "too busy" for this kind of work. The tyranny of the immediate must not be allowed to foreclose the developing of the future. We cannot assume that God will somehow mysteriously take care of this on His own. We are his "scouts."

Also, don't let yourself think that you're unworthy to be a model for younger servants of God. That can be a scary thought, I know. (Once I was sitting on the front row of the sanctuary, and I heard a squirmy seven-year-old

> **God calls us to lead not only with boldness but also with integrity and sensitivity.**

just behind say something to his mother. He had obviously been studying the fast-growing bald spot on the back of my head. "I want a haircut just like the pastor!" he announced.)

Young people today are not looking for us to appear a certain way so much as they want us to be genuine, to care about them, and to guide them closer to God's will. They don't really care what our stated age is. They want someone to follow.

Warren G. Bennis, well-known professor at Harvard Business School, published a book with an associate a few years ago titled *Geeks and Geezers: How Era, Values, and Defining Moments Shape Leaders.* In one section, they talk about an intriguing term you may not have heard, calling it "one of the most exciting ideas to emerge from our research."

> We discovered that every one of our geezers who continues to play a leadership role has one quality of overriding importance: neoteny. The dictionary defines *neoteny,* a zoological term, as "the retention of youthful qualities by adults." Neoteny is more than retaining a youthful appearance, although that is often part of it. Neoteny is the retention of all those wonderful qualities that we associate with youth: curiosity, playfulness, eagerness, fearlessness, warmth, energy. Unlike those defeated by time and age, our geezers have remained much like our geeks— open, willing to take risks, hungry for knowledge and experience, courageous, willing to see what the new day brings. Time and loss steal the zest from the unlucky, and leave them looking longingly at the past. Neoteny is a metaphor for the quality—the gift—that keeps the fortunate of whatever age focused on all the marvelous undiscovered things to come. . . .
>
> The capacity for "uncontaminated wonder," ultimately, is what distinguishes the successful from

the ordinary, the happily engaged players of whatever era from the chronically disappointed and malcontent. Therein lies a lesson for geeks, geezers, and the sea of people who fall in between.[26]

Who better to demonstrate neoteny than those of us who work for the King of kings! We've been given eternal life; we serve the One who promised to build His church regardless of the gates of Hades; He is the ultimate overcomer. We have absolutely no reason to be "chronically disappointed and malcontent" or to assume that the best days of the church are behind us. They are not. God is still raising up leaders.

I want to be part of that effort. I want to stay connected to the next generation of leaders. I've heard their cry for a church that offers what people need and expect. These young men and women sense better than most that people want *intimacy* (connecting with God), whereas most churches tend to give them only activity. People want to be *inspired* (faith expectation), while most churches are busy just improving the quality. People want to be *informed* (in order to grow), rather than to have an agenda pushed at them. People want *illustration* (modeling), not just marketing. People want to be *impacted* (to discover their spiritual gifts), which is far more vital than just developing programs. I'm committed to do everything I can to respond to their cry.

Along the way, I also get it . . . they don't want me to be *like* them. But they crave the experience and wisdom that the years have brought. They're looking for models.

While at a conference in 2007, Mark Batterson scouted out Jason Byars, a young church planter in Melbourne Beach, Florida. Mark knew I was planning a trip to Florida, so he asked me to contact Jason. Out of that has evolved a mentoring relationship that neither of us anticipated. We talk monthly.

Jason and his wife, Raina, want to hear life stories about managing the ups and downs of marriage, particularly for people in ministry . . . about the issues of faith struggles for pastors' children . . . and about enduring the stresses of pastoring. On a recent visit Jason said, "I want to learn, serve, and observe. Anyone who is being mentored has to do more listening than talking." He strongly suggested that people from his generation welcome the Elijah/Elisha model in their life.

One does not have to be perfect to be a mentor . . . just willing. I take it as a compliment when Jason says, "Bob, you've got 'elder-cool'!"

A legacy doesn't have to be monumental to be meaningful. It simply has to contribute to God's future. I love the line I picked up from Jeff Leake, a Pennsylvania pastor: "Leadership is not so much about what we do as about what we set in motion. It's about planting

**A legacy doesn't have to be monumental to be meaningful.**

the right seeds in people." Or, to change the metaphor, if you're pushing a big rock up a hill, you may think you're not accomplishing much . . . until you get it to the crest. Then you've set something in motion that can be pretty amazing.

I spoke in the beginning of this section about praying for God to raise up new workers in His harvest. When I was a Bible college student, I got the chance to speak at a Florida youth camp. The morning Bible teacher that week, J. Bashford Bishop, was a faculty member from another Bible college. As we talked one day, he asked me about my background. I mentioned that I had gone to Robert E. Lee High School in Jacksonville.

As soon as I said that, his eyes got big. "Really!" he exclaimed.

"Yes."

"And you're in the ministry today?"

"Yes," I answered. I thought maybe he had gone to our rival school, Andrew Jackson.

"What years did you go there?" he asked me.

I told him. Then he said, "That was about the time I pastored a little church right across the street—Riverside Assembly of God. It was a very tough pastorate. Not many people came . . . there was conflict in the church. I told the Lord one day, 'I'm really struggling here.'

"I felt as if God said to me in that moment, 'But you're here for a purpose. Why don't you focus on praying for those kids across the street?'

"So I would walk across the avenue at times and just put my hands on that chain-link fence, looking out at the athletic fields. I would say, 'Oh, God, would you touch some of these kids?'"

His eyes got misty at this point, realizing that I was one of those students. God was now giving this dear man a glimpse into what his faithfulness had produced. As I remember that conversation, I get choked up myself.

Not every great leader preaches to a church of thousands. Some are simply seers who zero in on a chain-link fence, and leave the results to God.

# Summary

# CHAPTER TWELVE

# Where Do You Stand?

**W**hat is your natural "face" as a leader? Which comes easiest to you?

On the other hand, which faces are *not* automatic for you, even though you know (after reading this book) that they are essential to the work of a Christian leader?

Here is a revealing tool to help you gain clarity on where you stand. It can help you know the unique person you are and what areas you need to address. As the old saying goes, "Most learning is accidental until you ask the right questions."

Answer each of the thirty-two questions honestly. Then do the simple math at the end. Finally, take the results into a time of "being still" before God, and ask Him how you can more closely follow the pattern of Jesus, leading with all four faces.

Read each statement and circle the number that best describes your position:

       1 – Not at all

       2 – Doubtful

       3 – Well, it depends . . .

       4 – Generally true of me

       5 – Absolutely

1. I enjoy hospital visitation.

    1    2    3    4    5

2. I get my own coffee (tea, etc.) in the morning.

    1    2    3    4    5

3. I make sure people's names are spelled correctly.

    1    2    3    4    5

4. I'm not afraid to propose something "outside the box."

    1    2    3    4    5

5. When someone tells me a prayer request, I have a system to make sure I remember it.

    1    2    3    4    5

6. If the custodian is out sick, I don't mind running a vacuum cleaner.

    1    2    3    4    5

7. I'm known as a peacemaker, a reconciler.

    1    2    3    4    5

8. I regularly read and listen to the ideas of younger generations.

    1    2    3    4    5

9. I think of myself as an example to the congregation.

    1    2    3    4    5

10. I don't have to prove the rightness of my viewpoint.

    1    2    3    4    5

11. I show up for meetings on time.

    1    2    3    4    5

12. I don't push my personal agenda and call it "vision."

    1    2    3    4    5

13. If God keeps me in this church for the rest of my active ministry, I'm okay with that.

    1    2    3    4    5

14. I don't mind if people call me by my first name (without a "Pastor" or "Rev." or "Dr." in front).

    1    2    3    4    5

15. I fully understand the church budget and do my best to abide by it.

    1    2    3    4    5

16. I have a clear sense of which things are not up for changing.

    1    2    3    4    5

17. I hang around after services to talk to people.

    1    2    3    4    5

18. If it snows on a Saturday night, I'll be out there helping clear the sidewalks early Sunday morning.

    1    2    3    4    5

19. I block out specific time each week for my family.

    1    2    3    4    5

20. I welcome healthy change.

    1    2    3    4    5

21. If a visiting speaker says something unbiblical, I find a way to correct it.

    1    2    3    4    5

22. I don't have a reserved parking space at church.

    1    2    3    4    5

23. I'm willing to delegate tasks that, in fact, I could do better myself.

    1    2    3    4    5

24. If we need a larger building, I'll not hesitate.

    1    2    3    4    5

25. When criticized, I somehow keep my cool.
    1    2    3    4    5

26. The "little people" in my church get featured along with those who are multi-talented.
    1    2    3    4    5

27. I can state my God-given mission in twenty-five words or less.
    1    2    3    4    5

28. I respect and use a wide variety of music styles.
    1    2    3    4    5

29. I return every message within one day.
    1    2    3    4    5

30. Occasionally I'll join the nursery team for a shift.
    1    2    3    4    5

31. I balance my personal checkbook every month.
    1    2    3    4    5

32. I'm always looking beyond the familiar crowd to those unreached.
    1    2    3    4    5

*Copy your numbers from the previous statements into the spaces below:*

1 \_\_  2 \_\_  3 \_\_  4 \_\_

5 \_\_  6 \_\_  7 \_\_  8 \_\_

9 \_\_  10 \_\_  11 \_\_  12 \_\_

13 \_\_  14 \_\_  15 \_\_  16 \_\_

17 \_\_  18 \_\_  19 \_\_  20 \_\_

21 \_\_  22 \_\_  23 \_\_  24 \_\_

25 \_\_  26 \_\_  27 \_\_  28 \_\_

29 \_\_  30 \_\_  31 \_\_  32 \_\_

*Now add vertically to get four totals:*

\_\_\_\_  \_\_\_\_  \_\_\_\_  \_\_\_\_
 A      B      C      D

# Result

Your "Face of a Shepherd" rating is (A):
_____ out of a possible 40

Your "Face of a Servant" rating is (B):
_____ out of a possible 40

Your "Face of a Steward" rating is (C):
_____ out of a possible 40

Your "Face of a Seer" rating is (D):
_____ out of a possible 40

# CHAPTER THIRTEEN

# You Can't Pick Just One

After I'd spoken at a conference for leaders under the age of forty, one person commented in the Q and A time, "I fit the face of a servant and steward, but I'm not as comfortable with the shepherd and seer. Is that okay?"

"Most people are motivated by one or two of the faces," I responded. "But it's important to embrace all of them."

Pastors can be servants (know how to wash feet)—but if they can't shepherd the flock or be a steward or a seer, their leadership is severely crippled. Or they can be an excellent steward (know how to count beans)—but if they're not up for the other three, they will again be hampered. Their church may run with impressive efficiency, but the people will not feel cared for.

I know a pastor who, in the pulpit, appears to truly care. He can hold a crowd spellbound. He's also good at managing/

**Christian leaders don't get the luxury of specialization.**

stewarding. At the same time, he sees the big vision. But don't try to talk to him one-on-one! You'll be very disappointed.

Christian leaders don't get the luxury of specialization. If we're going to follow the Jesus model, we can't say, "Well, my strong face is such-and-such . . . and the rest of the church staff will have to pick up the slack on the other three faces." We're leaders of people, not directors of programs. Mature leadership involves all four faces.

Personally speaking: My close colleagues tell me my strengths are as a shepherd and a seer. That simply means I have to work harder at being a servant and a steward. I can't pick just one—and neither can you.

As a matter of fact, "Researchers have shown across a variety of occupations and professions that only by working at what you cannot do can you expect to become the expert you aspire to be."[27]

## Day of Disaster

Let me illustrate by telling you about my friend Bob Farlow, who is not a pastor but instead is general manager of McGeorge Toyota a few miles from my house. Bob lives out his faith as a Christian leader in the marketplace. In that regard he, too, needs to be a shepherd, servant, steward, and seer to the people he serves.

He was getting ready for work one fateful morning back in late 2009 when he heard the *Today Show* announce that

Toyota had a huge problem: unintended acceleration, where cars would suddenly take off at high speed when the driver had done nothing to cause it. As a result, the company would have to recall millions of vehicles. Bob hadn't heard of such a problem at his local dealership—but regardless, he knew in that instant that his world would go absolutely crazy.

"I had faced other tough moments in business," he says, "but this was a 9/11 moment. I knew that as soon as I got to work, I'd be walking into a business war zone. The phones would be ringing off the hook. I would need to call my staff together immediately and instruct them on how to respond to this crisis."

But what would he say?

Still at home, Bob found a quiet place and sat still before God. His faith as a Christian anchored him in this moment. He reminded himself that even Jesus had once commented, "I don't speak on my own authority. The Father who sent me has commanded me what to say and how to say it" (John 12:49 NLT). Now in this hour, Bob asked for directions.

"I began to sense that the answer was, 'Take care of my people,'" he says. When I opened the staff meeting at eight o'clock, I repeated the question I had asked God: 'How can we best respond to this crisis?' The very first response from a manager was, 'We've got to take care of our customer's concerns.' This was a confirmation of what God had said to me in the time of being still an hour earlier.

"In the next minutes, I facilitated a strategic plan of action. On a whiteboard, we said that if the goal was to take care of our customers, we would do the following things:

- Provide loaner cars to those who needed them, at no rental charge.
- Take back any car we had sold within the last few weeks—no questions asked.
- Open our repair shop twenty-four hours per day, seven days a week.

"All of our employees unanimously agreed to step up to the plate and make this happen."

At the end of the staff meeting, a representative from corporate Toyota who happened to be present said, "That was incredible, Bob."

He responded, "You know I believe in God, right?"

The guest said, "Yes, I do." It turned into an opportunity to share how God was the primary source for personal guidance in leading this company.

Soon the local news media found out about the plan to open the service bays 24/7. Then the national media aired the story as well. Says Bob, "I thought to myself, *wow . . . I guess that's the end of my 'being still' for a while!*

**We must listen for God's instruction— then take appropriate action.**

"But I believed more than ever before that God can lead any of us when we take time to ask Him. I could have run this dealership off a cliff that day. It could have crashed and burned all of us. Instead, God saved the situation. And today, our business is better than ever."

# Before You Start Talking . . .

Listen to this, please. When you and I finally admit to ourselves and to God that we don't have all the answers . . . but we want them, He will guide us. We must be still and wait, however. We must listen for His instruction—then take appropriate action.

Says Bob: "Being still is something that gets noticed by those around you. Being still and checking in with Jesus gets you to the right priorities, the right answer, and the right actions to take."

Being still was the source of Bob Farlow taking up the face of a *shepherd*—caring for the people. He (and all his employees) had to become *servants,* adjusting their schedules to accommodate customer concerns. He showed the face of a *steward* by formulating a detailed plan. And along the way, he was also a *seer,* going completely outside the box to initiate 24/7 repair service. On this day, he didn't have the luxury of using just one "face." He needed all four.

This range of understanding was conceived in being still. What a valuable lesson for all Christian leaders.

I will close with three questions for you to ponder:

- Can "being still" increase the chances I will get it right, the way God wants me to do?
- If God wants to accomplish something for His people, do I believe He will settle for second best?
- Guess who I'm listening to when I'm still?

Here's a passage that fires me up every day of my life:

> Have you not known?
> Have you not heard?
> The everlasting God, the Lord,
> The Creator of the ends of the earth,
> Neither faints nor is weary.
> His understanding is unsearchable.
> He gives power to the weak,
> And to those who have no might He increases strength.
> Even the youths shall faint and be weary,
> And the young men shall utterly fall,
> *But those who wait on the Lord*
> Shall renew their strength;
> They shall mount up with wings like eagles,
> They shall run and not be weary,
> They shall walk and not faint.
>
> ISA. 40:28–31 NKJV, EMPHASIS ADDED

I want some of that strength, that power, that understanding *every single day* of my life. How about you?

Now you know how to get it. Be still and wait before God.

# Three Dads in the Shadows

### BY DEAN MERRILL

### (PUBLISHED IN *FOCUS ON THE FAMILY MAGAZINE*, JUNE 1997)

There was a lot that little Bobby Rhoden didn't know growing up.

All he knew was that he and Granny Cobb lived in a humble frame house along the railroad tracks in the dusty north Florida town of Olustee. They had a living room, a kitchen, one bedroom that the two of them shared, an outhouse, a hand pump in the back yard for water, kerosene lamps for light, and a garden.

But it was a spotlessly clean house—Granny made sure of that. And every Sunday she would take her grandson down to the nearby church, sometimes carrying an offering of home-grown vegetables or eggs from her chickens to supplement the meager tithe from their tiny government pension.

"I love you and I'll always take care of you," the bent little woman with the hair pulled back in a bun would tell Bobby, while holding him close on her lap. "Your momma—Martha Lee was what I named her—and your stepdaddy got killed back when you were only two years old. Got run over by a drunk driver down there along the highway while they were walking. I'll show you the spot sometime. . . . But God loves you, and I love you, and we'll make it somehow just fine."

World War II was over and the boy had started to school before he figured out what the word *stepdaddy* meant. The man who had been killed along with his mother was named Ashley Weeks—but the name Bobby wrote on his spelling papers was "Harold Robert Rhoden Jr." Where had he gotten that name?

"Well, your momma was married once before," Granny explained with sadness in her eyes. "She was awfully young, and there were problems. . . . Your dad—Harold Robert Rhoden Sr.—went and joined the Army during the war, when you were just a baby. . . . Nowadays he's off working. Maybe he'll come around sometime." And that was the end of the discussion.

Kids at school would ask Bobby, "Where's your dad?" and he, not wanting to have to clarify which one, would simply reply, "My dad died." The question seemed to come up fairly often, as if there were something behind their curiosity. Bobby didn't push matters. He wanted to fit in, to be a normal kid, to grow up in the usual way like everyone else.

Without a man in his life, Bobby learned from other kids how to play ball, and sometimes the town's older teenagers would take him fishing or to see a game at the high school. He felt very special whenever that happened, to be in the company of men.

His security was jostled at age twelve, when Granny Cobb's health began to plummet. The day came that her pledge to "take care of you forever" had to be adjusted; she went to live with a daughter, while Bobby—now growing tall enough to be called "Bob"—moved in with his Aunt Inez and Uncle E.D. In this home were other boys his age, and soon they were in high school together.

## Face to Face at Last

Then came the first shock. Bob was fifteen years old when, while visiting Granny Cobb in the hospital, an uncle pulled him aside and said, "By the way, your father just happens to be here in this same hospital, up on the fourth floor, with a back problem. Let me take you up to meet him."

Young Bob was nervous as he walked into the room and saw a good-sized man sitting on the edge of the bed, with reddish hair and freckles. *What do I call him?* He wondered. *Dad? ... Mr. Rhoden? ... Harold?—no, that wouldn't be respectful.* He didn't use any name in the end; he just stuck out his hand and said, "Hello."

Harold Robert Rhoden Sr. greeted him pleasantly, and the two talked for maybe twenty minutes. Young Bob asked where he lived. "We've got a place about thirty miles out of Jacksonville," the man replied. "I've got a wife and three kids now. When summer comes along, how about if I have you come out and spend a day with us?"

Bob's heart skipped a beat. "That would be great!" he answered. Maybe he would finally get to know this man whose name he bore.

They briefly discussed Granny Cobb's health, which was perilous, and then it seemed like there wasn't much else to talk about. Bob and his uncle wished the man a speedy recovery and left.

It was the last time Bob would ever lay eyes on the man. The phone never rang, nor did a letter ever arrive.

## Learning More

Bob Rhoden moved on toward adulthood the way he had grown up—rootless, alone, finding his own way in the world without fatherly counsel. He did come to terms with his heavenly Father, however, near the end of high school. Soon he sensed a calling to the ministry and enrolled in a Bible college. In time he met a young woman from Pennsylvania named Joan.

On their dates, they talked about family life—Joan's rich heritage of a loving dad and mom, a sister and a brother, and the contrasting vacuum in Bob's case. When they got to the stage of planning their wedding, they realized the groom's side of the sanctuary would have no relatives—only friends from college days.

Their early years together were spent at graduate school, and then they moved to start a new church in Richmond, Va., called West End Assembly of God. Joan said to her husband one day, "You know, it just feels to me like some pieces are missing in your family story. Next time we're in Florida, let's visit your aunt and try to find out more."

They did. When the question was raised, the aunt drew a long breath and then said, "Well, Bob, now that you're a grown man and married and everything . . . I should probably tell you that Harold Robert Rhoden Sr. is not your biological father after all."

The room suddenly lost all its air. "He's not?" Bob said in shock. "Then who is?"

She paused again, as if not wanting to dredge up unpleasant memories. "His name was Drew Strickland. He was a hired hand out at our farm, about eighteen or nineteen years old.

"When your mom turned up pregnant, the family was upset, of course; after all, she was only fourteen. Drew sort of disappeared, and Mom took little Martha Lee off to Jacksonville to live with another relative. That's where she met Harold, who felt sorry for her and also thought she was pretty. He decided he was willing to step in and give you a name. You were born ten days shy of her fifteenth birthday."

Bob and Joan could hardly speak from amazement. So that explained why Harold Rhoden hadn't followed through on his casual promise in the hospital to get better acquainted with Bob. The young teenager standing before him that day wasn't really his son after all. Harold had merely been continuing the disguise.

Presently Bob managed to ask, "Whatever happened to Drew Strickland?"

"He died around age thirty, due to heart problems. You were in grade school then."

Once again, the feelings of aloneness swept in. Granny Cobb had passed away, his mother had been struck down in the road, his true father was dead. . . . Only his wife now held him close and cherished him. And the church.

In the months and years that followed, the whole notion of *the family of God* became ever more precious to Bob Rhoden. People related not by blood but by the blood of Christ could become some of the closest and most caring people in his life. How wonderful that God had created the fellowship of believers in a cold and fractured world.

The church in Richmond grew over the next two decades, and meanwhile, Bob and Joan welcomed two daughters and a son into their home. From his wife, Bob learned much about how to be a sensitive and reliable parent.

That caring heart was evident in his public ministry as well. When he would preach about the love of God, audiences felt a tender spirit underneath the words. In 1991 he was elected superintendent of his denomination's Potomac District. The man without a father became father to some 315 churches across Virginia, West Virginia, Maryland and the District of Columbia.

## The Connection

But the Rev. Bob Rhoden still had not fully processed the depth of his fragmented past. In the summer of 1995, a letter from his aunt arrived saying that Harold Robert Rhoden Sr. had finally passed away. Suddenly Bob was plunged into reflection.

*The man who gave me life is dead—and I don't even have a picture of him.*

*The man who gave me a name is now dead. I saw him only once. And the man who gave me a future is dead.*

He and Joan traveled back to Florida, this time searching for any living relative of Drew Strickland. With considerable digging they found a brother. Bob placed a phone call, his hand trembling as he dialed. A man's voice answered.

"My name is Bob Rhoden, and I was wondering if maybe you could help me get a picture of my dad."

"Yes, I know about you," the voice quietly responded. "I've got some pictures, and in fact, I'd like to meet you. Could you come over to my place tomorrow?"

The next day Bob and Joan met a short, stocky man in a baseball cap who invited them into his apartment. The pictures he produced showed a face strikingly similar to Bob's. He kindly filled in various pieces of missing history.

Then Bob asked a question he had never voiced before. "Did my father ever marry?"

"Yes," the man replied. "In fact, he had three daughters before he died."

"So . . . are you saying I have three half-sisters I've never known about?"

"Yes, that's right."

In that moment, a wave of emotion swept over Bob Rhoden. For the first time in his life he felt *connected.* Here he was sitting in the living room of his real uncle, holding a faded photo of his real father and finding out he had real siblings. In some hard-to-explain fashion, he felt more like a person than in all his fifty-three years on earth.

Tears filled Bob's eyes as the man continued, "You know, I'm going to tell the girls about meeting you. They'd probably like to know all the rest, too."

In time, contacts were made, phone calls exchanged, and by early 1996, Bob met his three half-sisters. On Memorial Day 1996, an emotional family "reunion" occurred, with the younger generation present as well. They filled in the blanks of their heritage with laughter, stories, and tears. Close contact continues to this day.

## God of the Vacancies

Whenever Bob Rhoden tells his story from the pulpit these days, he pauses to give thanks for a mother who gave him life even under the most awful circumstances. "Somehow she resisted abortion. And as for my missing fathers," he goes on, "I've come to see that my personal history did not have to be a trap. Though my three dads were absent, God intervened in my life through my grandmother and others to prepare me for a future. That's the kind of God He is."

Audiences are riveted with the human drama of Bob's story and the spiritual lessons it portrays. They come up afterward with tears in their eyes to tell about missing persons in their own families. They ask questions about where to go from here, like the one woman who quietly said, "I have twins, and the man I'm married to is not their father. He knows that—*but they don't*. What should I do?"

Bob Rhoden kindly smiled and said, "I can't tell you what to do. But I would encourage you to be the one to open up the secret with them rather than waiting for them to find out. In this day and age of electronic databases and all the rest, they will probably get to the facts. Better for you to volunteer what happened than to be on the defensive later."

She nodded and said, "You know, I think they somehow suspect it anyway."

In a time when family structures are more shredded than ever, when family trees have extra branches sticking out in some places and gaping holes in others, Bob Rhoden's story shows a God who is flexible and resourceful. "He often steps into our lives before we even know we need Him," Bob says. "His attention and care never stray. No matter the past, there's hope for everyone."

# About the Author

While only two years old, Bob Rhoden lost both his parents to a car accident. He grew up with his widowed grandmother in a three-room house along a north Florida railroad track. By the time he reached age twelve, she was no longer able to keep caring for him, so he moved to nearby Jacksonville, where he lived with relatives until finishing high school.

This tenuous beginning, however, did not deter him from a fruitful future. Following graduation from Toccoa Falls Bible College (BA), he entered the ministry, serving two years alongside David Wilkerson, founder of Teen Challenge. He then became an associate of the well-known songwriter and pastor Ira Stanphill at a Pennsylvania church, during which time he also earned a second BA (Elizabethtown College) and met his wife, Joan.

Following completion of an MA (New Testament Studies) at Wheaton Graduate School outside Chicago, the young couple returned east to plant West End Assembly of God in Virginia's capital city—a church that experienced steady growth, mothered five other churches across the region, and built eighteen churches overseas. During this time, he published several articles in ministry journals and completed a DMin degree at nearby Union Presbyterian Seminary.

After twenty-two years, Bob's peers elected him superintendent of the Assemblies' Potomac District, guiding more than 300 churches for a fifteen-year period.

Today, he is a beloved mentor to young pastors and students; a well-received speaker at leadership conferences; he also serves on various boards and represents the Northeast Region on his denomination's Executive Presbytery. He and his wife are the proud parents of two daughters and a son, who have given them eight grandchildren.

# Endnotes

1. "One Solitary Life," sometimes attributed to James Allen Francis (1864–1928).
2. Gregory Knox Jones, *Play the Ball Where the Monkey Drops It: Why We Suffer and How We Can Hope* (San Francisco: HarperOne, 2001), 3–4.
3. Roy MacGregor, *Wayne Gretzky's Ghost* (New York: Random House, 2011), 3.
4. Andy Andrews, *The Traveler's Gift: Seven Decisions that Determine Personal Success* (Nashville: Nelson, 2002), 86
5. Andy Andrews, *The Noticer: Sometimes, All a Person Needs Is a Little Perspective* (Nashville: Thomas Nelson, 2009), 9.
6. James M. Kouzes and Barry Z. Posner, *The Truth about Leadership: The No-fads, Heart-of-the-Matter Facts You Need to Know* (San Francisco: Jossey-Bass, 2010), 31.
7. For more information about this ministry, go to: www.cleansingstream.org.
8. Kevin Leman and William Pentak, *The Way of the Shepherd: 7 Ancient Secrets to Managing Productive People* (Grand Rapids, MI: Zondervan, 2004), 87–89.

9. http://www.jewlicious.com/2007/01/teddy-kollek-97-father-of-modern-jerusalem.

10. Kouzes and Posner, *The Truth about Leadership,* 106–07.

11. This story was adapted from a video by Dr. Timothy George, Dean of Beeson Divinity School.

12. R. K. Greenleaf, *Servant Leadership: A Journey into the Nature of Legitimate Power and Greatness,* 25th anniversary edition (New York: Paulist Press, 2002), 23–24.

13. Juan Carlos Ortiz, *Disciple: A Handbook for New Believers* (Lake Mary, FL.: Creation House, 1995), 39.

14. E. Stanley Jones, *Abundant Living,* updated edition (Minneapolis: Summerside Press, 2010), May 18 entry.

15. Madeleine L'Engle, *A Live Coal in the Sea* (San Francisco: HarperOne, 1997), 167.

16. C. Gene Wilkes, *Jesus on Leadership: Discovering the Secrets of Servant Leadership from the Life of Christ* (Carol Stream, IL.: Tyndale, 1998), 166, 168.

17. http://www.google.com/about/company

18. Oswald Chambers, *My Utmost for His Highest,* updated edition (Grand Rapids, MI: Discovery House, 1992), reading for March 4; http://utmost.org/classic/could-this-be-true-of-me-classic/

19. Rick Warren, *The Purpose Driven Church: Every Church Is Big in God's Eyes* (Grand Rapids, MI: Zondervan, 1995), 111.

20. Tom Rees, *Break-through* (Waco, TX: Word, 1970),116–17.

21. Jim Collins, *Good to Great: Why Some Companies Make the Leap . . . and Others Don't* (New York: HarperBusiness, 2001).

22. C. S. Lewis, *Reflections on the Psalms* (New York: Harcourt, 1958), introduction.

23. James A. Belasco, *Teaching the Elephant to Dance: The Manager's Guide to Empowering Change* (New York: Penguin Books, 1991), back cover.

24. Gordon MacDonald, *Who Stole My Church?: What to Do When the Church You Love Tries to Enter the 21st Century* (Nashville: Thomas Nelson, 2008), 101. For a detailed account of the four change points, see 89–117.

25. Condensed from Alice Morse Earle, *The Sabbath in Puritan New England* (New York: Scribner, 1909), a public-domain book now posted at http://www.gutenberg.org/dirs/ etext05/8sabb10h.htm#15.

26. Warren G. Bennis and Robert J. Thomas, *Geeks and Geezers: How Eras, Values, and Defining Moments Shape Leaders* (Cambridge, Mass.: Harvard Business School Press, 2002), 20–21.

27. Kouzes and Posner, *The Truth about Leadership,* 132.

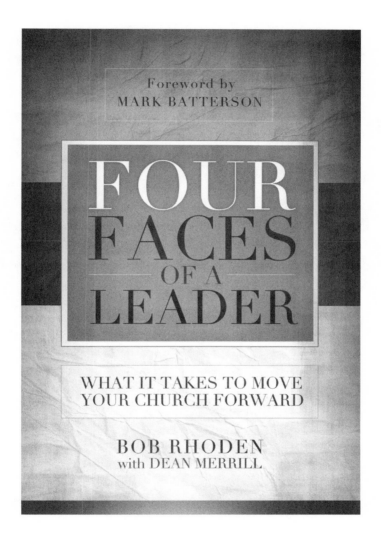